A Better Man, Husband, Father

Men can find the freedom to embrace the walk of a godly man through 180 short daily readings addressing the issues facing them in their spiritual journey.

Joe Miller

Copyright © 2015 by Joe Miller

A Better Man, Husband, Father
Men can find the freedom to embrace the walk of a godly man through 180 short daily readings addressing the issues facing them in their spiritual journey.
by Joe Miller

Printed in the United States of America.

ISBN 9781498438223

All rights reserved solely by the author. The author guarantees all contents are original and do not infringe upon the legal rights of any other person or work. No part of this book may be reproduced in any form without the permission of the author. The views expressed in this book are not necessarily those of the publisher.

www.xulonpress.com

Endorsements:

Greg Bowman: Pastor and Author
In a world that moves at the speed of life, "A Better Man" causes us to slow down and think. Joe's observations about his own life will give you new insights into your own. His authentic, grace-filled writing style match the way he lives out his life – seeking new ways every day to be "A Better Man."

Dustin Richie: Warehouse Supervisor for a national Logistics company
It was such a nice read, I enjoyed how he didn't "tell" the reader what to do, those books are so intimidating, he speaks to the reader like a friend. I love the "Bottom Line Thought".

Dr. Gordon Venturella, CFRE: VP of University Advancement at Lincoln Christian University, Lincoln, IL; His rich background includes working with a variety of non-profits, higher education, mega-churches, and international relief organizations.

Joe is totally transparent – mucho masculine – preeminently practical – a giver of grace. The writing is clear, honest and spiritual without being preachy. Perfect men need not bother reading. Broken men who want to be better – men like Joe and me – will be inspired just a few pages in.

Michael Aukofer, DMA: Composer, Arranger & Musical Director, Producer Songwriter & Teacher, and Worship Leader.

Joe hits the nail on the head (or thumb); progress, not perfection is all we can strive for in this journey of life we are all traveling.

Table of Contents

Introduction xiii
Dedication... xv
Acknowledgements..xvii

Day 1:   The Man In The Mirror 19
Day 2:   Who Are You?...20
Day 3:   The Comeback Trail 21
Day 4:   God Has A Sense Of Humor 22
Day 5:   Under Construction 23
Day 6:   Sounds Like A Plan 24
Day 7:   A Love Letter 25
Day 8:   Stuck With Skeletons, 1 26
Day 9:   Stuck With Skeletons, 2 27
Day 10: Stuck With Skeletons, 3 28
Day 11: Stuck With Skeletons, 4 29
Day 12: Who Am I? 30
Day 13: Married Man, Or Partner?...........................31
Day 14: Unwanted Christmas Gifts 32
Day 15: Absorbing Little Guys.................................33
Day 16: Our Complaint Meter 34
Day 17: 4 Eyes..35
Day 18: Are We Just Saying It?................................36
Day 19: Easy? Yeah, right.......................................37
Day 20: About That Prayer Thing..............................38
Day 21: 5 Simple Truths...39
Day 22: Michael Jordan 40
Day 23: Use Your Imagination 41
Day 24: Follow The Dog 42
Day 25: The Repairman 43
Day 26: Where Are You Looking? 44
Day 27: Stones And Glass Houses.............................45
Day 28: What If?...46
Day 29: Sliced Bread...47
Day 30: I Hate That...48
Day 31: Thin Slicing...49
Day 32: Troubled Sleep 50
Day 33: Grasp His Hand 52

Day 34:	Unhappy?	53
Day 35:	Gifts	54
Day 36:	None But Us	55
Day 37:	Burning Embers	56
Day 38:	Indian Lore	57
Day 39:	God's Top 10 List	58
Day 40:	The Brain Shelf	59
Day 41:	Thanks Man!	60
Day 42:	The Big Boy Pants	61
Day 43:	Obituary-itis	62
Day 44:	The Right Man	63
Day 45:	Attaboy	64
Day 46:	First Class Mail	65
Day 47:	Smokey Robinson	66
Day 48:	Identity Theft	67
Day 49:	Good Theater	68
Day 50:	Bridges And Barriers	69
Day 51:	Who Needs A Flashlight When...	70
Day 52:	Quirks	71
Day 53:	8 Simple Things	72
Day 54:	Birds Of A Feather	73
Day 55:	Racism Is Red	74
Day 56:	Sanity On Sunday	75
Day 57:	Special Silliness	76
Day 58:	The Word Demon	77
Day 59:	Two Options	78
Day 60:	No U-Hauls	79
Day 61:	The Dog Park	80
Day 62:	Jacked Up On Jesus	81
Day 63:	Eight Groaks	82
Day 64:	Friends	83
Day 65:	Resentments	84
Day 66:	Those Pesky Thoughts	85
Day 67:	Notes	86
Day 68:	Twin Fetus's	87
Day 69:	Just A Second!	88
Day 70:	You Can't Close That Door	89
Day 71:	Excuses & Responsibility	90
Day 72:	Wrestling With God	91
Day 73:	Getting Up For It	93
Day 74:	This Too Shall Pass	94

Day 75:	Real Men Are Humble	95
Day 76:	The Monkeys in Our Lives	96
Day 77:	Good, Better, Best	97
Day 78:	Folsom Prison Blues	98
Day 79:	Truth In Advertising	99
Day 80:	Grackles	100
Day 81:	Money	101
Day 82:	A Flat Tire	102
Day 83:	Potato Or Egg?	103
Day 84:	Dear Porn Daddy	104
Day 85:	A Door Stop	106
Day 86:	I've Got Your Back	107
Day 87:	Never Gonna Win!!	108
Day 88:	Well?	109
Day 89:	Walls	110
Day 90:	Life-ism's	111
Day 91:	Seasons	112
Day 92:	Broken Crayons	113
Day 93:	Goose Church	114
Day 94:	What's New?	115
Day 95:	The Perfect Marriage	116
Day 96:	Dumping	117
Day 97:	One Sided Conversation	118
Day 98:	A Fool and His Money	119
Day 99:	Drop It	120
Day 100:	To-Do Lists	121
Day 101:	Every.Single.Day !!	122
Day 102:	Our Words	123
Day 103:	Fish Swimming Upstream	124
Day 104:	Surprise !	125
Day 105:	And In This Corner...	126
Day 106:	Frienemies (fren-uh-mees)	127
Day 107:	Healing Wanted	128
Day 108:	What About The Kids?	129
Day 109:	Good Enough	130
Day 110:	Ordinary	131
Day 111:	Happiness	132
Day 112:	Stale Bread And Crackers	133
Day 113:	How Hard Is It?	134
Day 114:	Making Change	135
Day 115:	Go Ahead And Do It	136

Day 116:	What's The Point?	137
Day 117:	Living The Good Life	138
Day 118:	America	139
Day 119:	Boldness	140
Day 120:	Just One	141
Day 121:	Real Friends Are Real	142
Day 122:	Liberal Logic	143
Day 123:	Public Enemy # 1	144
Day 124:	Evil Will Not Win	145
Day 125:	50-20 Vision	146
Day 126:	The Train	147
Day 127:	Reactions	148
Day 128:	We're Gardeners	149
Day 129:	Straight Arrow	150
Day 130:	Stress	151
Day 131:	The Hard Question	152
Day 132:	Oxygen	153
Day 133:	Give Up And Give	154
Day 134:	Fairy Tales	155
Day 135:	The Butler Did It	156
Day 136:	You Never Know	157
Day 137:	A Blood Bath	158
Day 138:	Figure It Out	159
Day 139:	School Of Hard Knocks	160
Day 140:	The Marriage Box	162
Day 141:	Men And Boys	163
Day 142:	A Matter Of Perspective	164
Day 143:	The Beast Within: Anger	165
Day 144:	The Beast Within: Greed	166
Day 145:	The Beast Within: Laziness	167
Day 146:	The Beast Within: Pride	168
Day 147:	The Beast Within: Lust	169
Day 148:	The Beast Within: Envy	170
Day 149:	The Beast Within: Gluttony	171
Day 150:	Death	172
Day 151:	Things He Doesn't See	173
Day 152:	When The Planes Stopped Flying	174
Day 153:	Truck Drivers	175
Day 154:	A Child's Prayer	176
Day 155:	A Little Extra Light	177
Day 156:	The Starfish Story	178

Day 157:	We Don't Know	179
Day 158:	Why A Christian?	180
Day 159:	In A Rut	181
Day 160:	Out Of The Rut	182
Day 161:	12 Simple Things	183
Day 162:	I'm Sorry	184
Day 163:	Woman	185
Day 164:	Whining	186
Day 165:	Be Very, Very Careful	187
Day 166:	What Gets Lost	188
Day 167:	Yes	189
Day 168:	Right Now	190
Day 169:	Angel Of Apathy	191
Day 170:	I Ate The Whole Thing	192
Day 171:	If Those Walls Could Talk	193
Day 172:	George Carlin	194
Day 173:	Turn The Heat Down	195
Day 174:	Irritants	196
Day 175:	A Tough Issue	197
Day 176:	For The Women	198
Day 177:	Some Life-ism's	199
Day 178:	Living Large	200
Day 179:	Where Are You Going?	201
Day 180:	Who Is He?	202

Epilogue 204

Introduction
A Better Man, Husband, Father

The following paragraph offers a great description of what a perfect man, husband, and farther is;

That short paragraph tells us that there is no such thing as a perfect man, husband, and father. Perfection is not obtainable because we are all human. We're all flawed in some areas of our lives. At times we may not readily recognize those flaws. Sometimes our lives won't be in sync with how God made us to be.

Wherever we are in our lives, there is room for improvement. Being good enough is not an option. Striving and working to be a better man, husband and father is our only option if we are going to be all that God intends us to be. As men, when we look deeply within ourselves, we yearn to be better at what we do and who we are. In our gut we realize that something isn't quite right. We feel emptiness, or sense a hole in our heart, and know we are a bit off kilter.

The first step to begin dealing with the yearning is to recognize that life is a journey. It's a process, not an event. It won't always be enjoyable, carefree, and painless. It's work. At times it will seem as if we are taking two steps forward then falling back one step. We may do that two step-one step dance in our lives every day as we continue to pursue spiritual growth.

A Better Man, Husband, Father will enable men to recognize their yearnings to be better men, and will help them grasp the idea that it's a process. It's a book which provides 180 short, easily read blue collar, grass roots articles of everyday life situations which affect us all in our relationships. That includes our relationship with God, the One who has His hand in our lives. He knows it is a process, and He is patient as we experience the two steps forward, one step back dance in our journey. From the worst to the best He is there for all of us to be our guide and our encouragement.

Enjoy the journey, you have chosen. It will make you a better you, one that will be pleasing to God, because you matter to Him so much.

Dedication

This book is dedicated to my daughter Gretchen. She's known me at my worst, my best, and everywhere in between. Where I am today in this journey of doing life is, in great part, a result of her faithfulness to God in following His leadings as He placed His hand on her heart to do what was needed, when it was needed. She was a pencil in God's hand as she provided the gentle pokes and prodding necessary to begin the turn of this guy from a very broken man into a follower of Christ.

Acknowledgements

Many men shared tables with me in church basements on week nights and weekends years ago. They, and particularly Tom, shared some profound wisdom and tough love about this thing we call doing life. They walked alongside me as I morphed from being a fantastic drunk into a man who could begin to grasp that there was a spiritual side of my being. I thank all of those anonymous men.

I deeply thank my family who patiently stood beside me throughout years of struggle. They shared my pain and withstood their own by sticking with me to provide the support that I needed so much during those rough times and beyond.

I humbly thank all of the guys in the small groups I have been in at churches. Their transparency as men has encouraged and strengthened my spiritual growth as a Christ follower. Their example has shown me that while we are so different, we are all remarkably the same

I cannot go without thanking the Pastors at my church, Greg, Darren, Gordon, and visiting Pastor Tim for helping me fully realize the immeasurable amount of grace and love that God has for this man, and for the forgiveness and redemption He has given me. It is through their teachings that I rejoice in that knowledge and am thankful that I am not the man I used to be as I continue to grow in the Lord.

As a lover of music, I thank Michael, a dear friend and the leader of our worship team which faithfully, every Sunday, does what it does best. His team provides the music that reaches so deeply within me, softens my heart, and opens it to the teachings I am about to hear.

Finally, I have special thanks for a dear friend and mentor, Norm Whitney. Norm knows everything about me, and he loves me. It's Norm who walked me through all of my past and was able to get through to me that God's hand has always been in my life whether I recognized it or not, whether I wanted it or not. It was through that lesson and his example, that I was able to free myself of the guilt I was carrying over my past and accept the full force of God's love for me. Norm has been such an encourager, has offered so much hope and joy, and he has never let go. He is the brother I never had.

Day 1:
The Man In The Mirror

When I look in the mirror
who do I see?
Do I see a stranger,
or do I see me?
Is the man that I see there
loving and kind,
or does he stare back
with a troubled mind?
One thing I'm sure of
as I stand there and stare,
if it's not me I'm seeing
I'd best turn to prayer.
It's a sign I've lost hold of
some things to hold dear,
like being more Christ-like,
and keeping Him near.
If I can't be happy
seeing me in my skin
it means I am living
with way too much sin.

Joe Miller, 2012

Day 2:
Who Are You?

How would you answer that question?
Suppose others were asked who you are:
How would your wife answer it?
How would your children answer it?
How would your co-workers answer it?
How would your friends at church answer it?
How would God answer it?

Would the answers to those questions be consistent, or would they vary depending on who asked? Would the answers be different because of differing ways you project yourself to others? How do you project yourself to others?

It's not who you are, it's <u>whose</u> you are

Living as a follower of Christ isn't always easy. Are you consistently trying to live as one of God's children, or is it an on again-off again effort? If it's not a consistent effort is it because you are trying to portray yourself differently to different people? Jesus was consistent in all that He did. The Bible is full of wonderful examples of Jesus, the man. Getting into the word and regularly talking with Him are 2 of the ways to begin the work toward achieving consistency in all that you do and in all of your relationships.

Bottom Line Thought: If your emphasis is on who you are rather than whose you are, are you ready to take the steps toward becoming more real as you travel the long dirt road of life?

Day 3:
The Comeback Trail

We hear a lot about the comeback trail. It's talked about when an athlete comes back to a team following an injury (he's on the comeback trail), or politicians running for office when their ratings start to rise. We never hear it referencing just average guys like you and I. I Goggled the term to see if there was or is such a place and got no results from that search. It's a term that got coined somewhere along the line that is used for situations where one is making a comeback from some adversity.

We have all probably heard of a term used to identify our journey through life, "that long dirt road of life." I like that term, not because my life is dirty, but because it speaks to me as it paints a realistic picture of my spiritual journey.

- It's not a freeway ride which I can just sail along on
- It can be rough, have twists and turns, and there are unknown surprises along the way
- It's a one way road that takes me from where I am now to my final destination
- At the end, my final destination, it opens up to an eternity where I will meet my Lord.

Because we are not perfect beings, as we travel down that road there are times when we make false turns. We get lost, and we stray. I have strayed and gotten lost several times and with help have found my way to the comeback trail that eventually intersected with, and ended at, the long dirt road.

The comeback trail also speaks to me through a picture in words:

- It's a do-over, one of the wonderful things God gives us
- It's where we find the grace that God floods us with
- It's where we find forgiveness in abundance
- It's where we are redeemed and restored.

Isn't it great news to realize that regular guys just like you and I can hit the comeback trail?

Bottom Line Thought: In your travel down the long dirt road of life, have you made some wrong turns? Did you find the comeback trail? Have you tasted the grace, forgiveness, and redemption that comes with the comeback trail?

Day 4:
God Has A Sense Of Humor

We have always had a dog as part of our family. Whenever one went to "The Rainbow Bridge", we have been able to "rescue" another pooch and welcome him into our home. Dog lovers fully understand how a dog can steal your heart. We have always had a special bond with our dogs.

It is that special bond between man and dog that makes me believe that they really are man's best friend. There are certain characteristics about a dog that makes that bond as strong as it is:

- They love us unconditionally.
- They are extremely loyal and faithful to us.
- They always protect us.
- They are very patient with us.
- They are constant companions.
- They are happy when we are connected with them.
- Our faults don't diminish their love for us.
- They aren't biased or prejudiced.
- They are very forgiving.
- They give us their all.

In going through that list, I don't see any characteristic that I shouldn't have as a man. In fact, they are the same characteristics that God has, ones He has shown me over and over throughout my life. He has shown them through His word and His son Jesus. They are the traits I should have as a child of God. I, unlike my dog, fall short of them far too many times in my life. What a lesson my dog can teach me.

So what does this have to do with God having a sense of humor? Is it possible that God, in His infinite wisdom, planned for dogs to be man's best friend all along so that we would always have those God like characteristics right under our noses? And isn't it ironic that man's best friend is God spelled backwards?

Bottom Line Thought: Are the characteristics you have as a man in sync with the lesson we can learn from dogs?

Day 5:
Under Construction

In Illinois we jokingly say we have two seasons here--winter and construction. At times I wondered if Illinois didn't own more orange cones and barrels than all other states combined. That changed when my daughter and her family moved to Kentucky and I took trips to visit them. Interstate 65 into Louisville always seems to be under construction. Being the principal route south for commerce, many, many 18 wheelers use it. Traveling that route has become a character builder to say the least. I find that as I drive that route, my character is often tested to its limits.

Our character is who we are. I Googled "list of character traits" once and got a list of 66 words that are character traits. When my character was tested in the above travel tale, I found that 39 out of those 66 traits were involved. That speaks of how much work my character building needs. You see, my character is not only who I am, but what others see of me. Yes, I can, and do, mask my character, and I can hide it as well, but in the long run my true character will be known by those who know me best.

As we travel down the road of life we are constantly in the process of building and improving upon our character. Just as in construction zones, it's not always an easy process to navigate. In building character we run into stumbling blocks, unexpected surprises, hardships, pain, grief, sorrow, and our own flaws. One thing about character building is always true: it is a continuing learning process of getting to know who we really are and who we really want to be as men.

> **CONSTRUCTION ZONE**
> **PROCEED AT OWN RISK**

Men who are Christ followers, no matter where they are in their journey, will not have to use as much caution as those who are not. God is paving the way for us and all we have to do is trust Him as we follow where He is leading.

Bottom Line Thought: Have you discovered a need for construction and rebuilding of some of the traits of your character? What do others see in your character? Are they seeing your true character?

Day 6:
Sounds Like A Plan

Plans are a part of our lives. There are always plans to be made or followed.

- We make plans for our retirement.
- Builders follow plans when building structures.
- We make wedding plans for our daughters.
- We make vacation plans for our families.
- We plan our work so we can work our plan and be efficient and effective.

The purpose of plans is to ensure that things are done properly and in a workable order so that the end result will stand the test of time. If a builder doesn't follow the plan that the architect made the home he is building may not be structurally or aesthetically sound. Something will be wrong. The builder, in doing that, is exerting control over the job that he really has no authority doing. If changes in the plan are necessary, a good builder will consult with the architect before making those changes.

We regularly come up with plans about how we want our lives to run their course don't we? When I make plans for my life, I am sure that I am so good at it that my life will run perfectly smoothly. We all like to feel that we are in control of our lives. When the plans we make for our lives get disrupted, we don't react very well do we? We don't like not being in control of our lives. We often forget that our lives have a grand architect. He is God.

God has a plan for our lives because He knows what is best for us, and how we will be used for His kingdom work. His plans for us aren't written on a blueprint that we can see. To know what His plan is for us, he has shown us how to talk with Him, and all He asks is that we listen to Him and trust Him. He asks that we be open to His leadings. His plan may not be the same as our plan, but it will always be a better plan for us. His plan may be quite different than the smooth plan we tend to make, but it is the right plan.

Bottom Line Thought: The only plan we need for our lives is to follow God's plan. Do you have plans for your life that are not clearly acceptable to what God's plan might be? Do you listen regularly to the architect of your life, God?

Day 7:
A Love Letter

I came upon across a news story about love letters. A husband had written love letters to his girlfriend years ago. He married her and kept writing her love letters. After 40 years of marriage he found that she had carefully saved all the letters in labeled and orderly boxes in the attic. When asked about it they both talked about how much they enjoyed going back to those old love letters periodically.

In those times love letters were special and unique. Why?

- They painted a word picture of what was going on in the life of the writer.
- The letters were full of passion, descriptive adjectives, and details.
- The happiness of the author and the recipient was a strong theme throughout.
- They shared thoughts of love and hope for the future.
- Since they were very personalized, a strong bond was a result.

In today's world, love letters are almost a thing of the past. Even if there were such a thing it would probably be an e-mail or worse yet, a short tweet or a text message. A bolder person might put it on Facebook for the world to see. I am admittedly old-fashioned, but I don't see how those social media love letters are very personal. I wonder how many folks actually sit down at the keyboard and compose one using a document program, and then mail it. And, it would be a surprise if someone took the time to physically write one in long hand with pen and paper.

We have the longest love letter available to us every day of our lives. Is it a radical thought to consider the Bible as a love letter from God to us? After all, it speaks of:

- His love for us throughout, either directly or through example or lessons taught.
- His concern for our well being
- His protection for us
- His promises to us who have chosen to follow Jesus.

Bottom Line Thought: What might be some changes in your heart if you looked at the bible as a love letter instead of a book of rules, conditions, history, and out of date stories? After all, it is God's word, and it comes only out of His love for us.

Day 8:
Stuck With Skeletons, 1

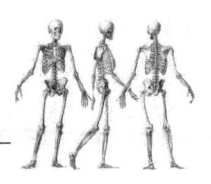

If your past is poisoning your present and future, you are stuck with some skeletons. It gets noisy and crowded in that closet of the mind where the skeletons are stored. The skeletons we have are as varied as our imagination will allow. Sometimes we like to bring one or two of them out of the closet to massage them, think about them, mope over them. They fill us with grief, shame, guilt, and unhappiness. When they are all rattling around in our head, we end up in a bad way don't we?

Let's give those skeletons some names:

- Past failures
- Our indiscretions
- Our mistakes
- Times when we have been hurt or slighted
- Resentments or anger over past stuff in our lives
- Current sin we just can't let go of

If we fail to deal with the skeletons, we will never be the men we are meant to be. It will not be possible because those skeletons will play a role in the decisions and choices we make and will jade our thoughts. It is incumbent that we cremate those skeletons and then let the ashes of our past go. *Only then will we be able to live free and joyfully pursue the full walk with Christ.*

Step 1 in getting unstuck from the skeletons is to <u>accept our past</u>. Our past doesn't have to be our baggage. Our past is our very own unique story. It is what has brought us from where we were to where we are today, wherever that is. Our past is us, uniquely in our skin. There is nothing that any of us can do to change that. It is as much a part of us as our DNA. By accepting our past we are free to not let that past, no matter how bad it is, control us and dictate who we are today, or who we will be tomorrow.

What do we do with the past we accept? We <u>embrace it</u>. By accepting it and embracing it, we come to peace with it, we understand that it *was me and <u>is not me now</u>*. Through that understanding, we cross the River Calm. Our future can now become greater than our past.

Bottom Line Thought: Will you walk with God to the River Calm as you dump your skeletons?

Day 9:
Stuck With Skeletons, 2

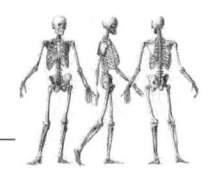

Getting unstuck from our skeletons is a progressive work:

Step 1: We need to accept and embrace them.

Once we have come to the River Calm by accepting and embracing our past, we're ready to take the next step if we're serious about getting unstuck from the skeletons. Step 2 isn't always that easy to do, or to continue to do. We have to <u>leave our past in the past</u>. We've got to drop the baggage on the other side of the riverbank. We've previously acknowledged that we're carrying the skeletons, now it's time to let them go. It's time to say bye-bye to them, to refuse to bring them out from the closet of the mind.

What happens when we pick at a scab on our arm? It re-opens the wound and interrupts the healing process. The more we pick the scab, the longer it remains an unhealed wound. When the impulse to pick on the scabs that are our skeletons becomes strong, it is time to change the channel or turn off that big flat screen that is our mind. It's not the time to go get the popcorn or set the DVR.

We can NEVER change our past. We can only change our future. That will never happen as long as we don't stop picking at the scab, refuse to change the channel, or leave the past in the past where it belongs....on the shore of the River Calm.

God didn't create us to be masseurs who continually massage our pasts. He created us to make good choices with the full knowledge that we would make bad ones along the way. He knew those bad choices would create those skeletons of our minds. He also knew that we could learn from those choices and make positive changes in our lives, changes that would strengthen our walk with the Lord. Those changes are made easier by leaving our past in the past.

Bottom Line Thought: Can you start to place your past in the past by dropping the suitcase? Are you ready to let healing begin by not picking at the scabs of those wounds?

Day 10:
Stuck With Skeletons, 3

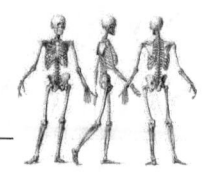

Getting unstuck from our skeletons is a progressive work:

> Step 1: We need to accept and embrace them.
> Step 2: We need to leave our past in the past.

Now that we're starting to get serious about our efforts to quit dancing with the stars, er, skeletons, what is the next logical step in getting unstuck from the skeletons? A quick definition of one word will provide a good clue. That word is insanity. When I was an active drunk years ago, I was sure I was going insane, and I told a good friend that. He described insanity as *repeating the same mistake over and over again, each time expecting a different result*.

Addictive sins fall directly in that category of skeletons. We tend to keep feeding those skeletons until we know we need to change our lives, and we keep feeding them even after we know we need to change. There is only one way to get unstuck from them: We have to <u>stop repeating past mistakes</u>. That can be difficult to do. Here are some thoughts that will help break that chain:

- We have to understand and accept that it will not be easy.
- We need to know that it will take time and there may be miss-steps.
- Victory will occur only through a series of small victories.
- We need to embrace and hold on to each of them as we work toward total victory.
- We need to focus on those small victories instead of accepting the guilt that comes from the failures.

There is something we can do to help us in the process. We set boundaries on ourselves. We need to think in terms of protecting ourselves from ourselves. We build boundaries around each of those repetitive behaviors which have or will become a part of our skeleton collection and then consistently remind ourselves not to cross that boundary to get to the behavior. In doing so we are building a mindset that it is our boundaries that will define us, not our skeletons. It becomes a one on one battle. God is a loyal and faithful ally when we begin to set boundaries to protect ourselves.

Bottom Line Thought: As a man who is working to improve himself, are you looking at boundaries you can set?

Day 11:
Stuck With Skeletons, 4

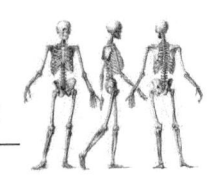

Getting unstuck from our skeletons is a progressive work:

>Step 1: We need to accept and embrace them.
>Step 2: We need to leave our past in the past.
>Step 3: We need to stop repeating past mistakes.
>Step 4: We need to expand our borders.

The final step of getting unstuck from our skeletons is to <u>expand our borders</u>. In the previous step we established that if we build boundaries around our behaviors we will have built a fence to remind us not to go near the behavior. Now that the boundaries are it place, we can pull on the full strength of our Lord to enable us to expand those so that they become borders. Each time we are approaching a border we will have help to allow us to say to ourselves "nope, I'm not going to go there." The more we do that, the easier it will become. The trick to getting unstuck is to expand those borders on a regular and continuing basis. By doing that we are separating ourselves further and further away from those things which will produce skeletons.

Success in starting to move the borders will allow us to focus more on the future with diminishing glances back to the closet that holds the skeletons. A side effect will be less inclination on our part to even go toward the boundaries and we will find ourselves looking at the skeletons less. We will not forget they are there, we will simply choose not to see them. As the borders have expanded we are becoming new men, and we will start to appreciate the skeletons because it is them that has driven us to become those new men. We are in the process of building a whole new past at this point, and we are free to move on to become stronger Christ followers as God intended us to be. We will have become empowered by our success because we took on our worst enemy, ourselves, and won.

Bottom Line Thought: Are the skeletons in your closet stopping you from being the man you can be? Are you now prepared to fight those skeletons and win? Is anything stopping you from taking on that fight?

Day 12:
Who Am I?

"The person I am is the parts I play"

Source unknown

God made each of us unique beings. Because of that, as His children we are all special in our own individual ways. He didn't give us roles to play to mask who He made us to be. He gave us a life to live so that we can fully praise Him and bask in all of His glory and serve at His will for the betterment of all mankind. That life isn't a play. It's real life, and yet we spend a lot of our time wearing masks or playing parts *we* want to play. Sometimes we don't want to be as God made us, and we don't want to live our lives as He intended us to. When we wear our masks and play the parts we want to play it's really just all about us isn't it?

How much simpler and joy filled would our lives be if we could honestly say "the person I am is the real me, the one with no masks and no roles to play"?

Bottom Line Thought: How much better would we be as men if we dropped the masks and refused to play roles?

Day 13:
Married Man, Or Partner?

A good marriage partner will always

> love you the way you are
> be a caring parent to children
> be sensitive to your needs and build you up
> be diligent in all financial matters
> be truthful, honest, and not cheat on you
> appreciate your intelligence and be proud of you
> encourage you in all you do and respect you
> be a part of and help you in your spiritual journey

Those are some of the qualities of a marital relationship that play key roles in helping marriages sustain themselves and grow. They have passed the test of time.

When we decided it was time to get married, did we shop for a married couple's owner manual? There are many good programs, seminars, books, and counseling sessions available that engaged couples can use, read, or attend prior to tying the knot, and some are a requirement for marriage. But, because of the youth, passion, and normal commotion that are a part of the whole romance to marriage dynamic, it is really just a guess to know *exactly* how the couple will relate to each other as their marriage becomes "routine" over time. It is then that the partners start discovering that marriage isn't the cakewalk, or as blissful, as they might have thought it would be.

Whenever there are 2 folks together, there will be differences. Marriage is no exception. In marriage there will be failed expectations, dreams and hopes that were born of rose colored glasses, fluttering love shrouded hearts, and awe clouded minds. When that happens, it's "welcome to the real world" time for the couple. There will be stumbling blocks that present themselves, choices and decisions to be made, and many new discoveries that, in any combination can erode the solidarity of the marital relationship. It is each partner's reaction to, and the methods they deal with those, that will determine the strength of the marriage for time to come.

Taking mutual ownership of the time tested qualities of a marital relationship will provide the backbone needed for safe passage through the real world of marriage.

Bottom Line Thought: Whether engaged, newly married, or in a long term marriage, do you have the good marriage partners list of tools as your guide for a sound marriage?

Day 14:
Unwanted Christmas Gifts

At Christmas time many of us lie. That's right; we lie and fib. We do it within the context of being nice. Some might think we lie on that occasion out of political correctness. However, lying is lying isn't it? What is it about Christmas that brings out the liar in many of us? The answer to that is, simply, because it's Christmas.

The exchange of gifts at Christmas is a tradition (or maybe an obligation for some). The lying is about those unwanted or unneeded gifts. We don't know when we gift someone if it is an unwanted or unneeded gift. On the flip side, when we receive an unwanted or unneeded gift, the giver doesn't know either, do they? The receivers of gifts seldom say what they really think if the gift they received is either unwanted or unneeded. No one says "Oh, that's ugly", or, "why did you give me this, you know I'll never use it". Instead, we say, perhaps unenthusiastically, things like "wow, that is really nice", or "I've always wanted something like that." Enter, re-gifting, or shelves, or garbage cans, or Goodwill. It happens year in and year out.

Something of far more importance happens at the same time each year. It's the time of the year that we are reminded once again that God's gift to all of us is His son Jesus. It's the gift that was given to us all to save us. It's a gift we can choose to embrace or reject. It's a gift that some reject or treat just like an unwanted Christmas gift. Sadly, they don't see that gift, the one that represents life, as little more than some junk wrapped in a pretty box. They ignore it or just pay soft lip service to it.

Bottom Line Thought: How do you look at and treat the greatest gift you ever received, Jesus? Is He sometimes thought of as unwanted, in the way, something to be put on a shelf, or something to look at just once in a while? Or did you receive that gift with pure honest joy and thankfulness and share it with others through all that you are say and do?

Day 15:
Absorbing Little Guys

Natural sponges are great for lots of things. One of the features of a natural sponge is that when used, they absorb an incredible amount of water. A small tennis ball size natural sponge will expand to the size of a softball or bigger when used to wash the car. I remember how thrilled I was when, as a small child, we would take a day trip to go to Tarpon Springs, FL to see the divers in the sponge boats come in from harvesting sponges.

Our kids are a lot like sponges, especially when they are young and haven't developed selective hearing yet. They *hear everything* we, as parents, say whether we think they are hearing it or not. Oh, and they also see everything we do. Not only do they absorb those things, it is not uncommon for them to parrot those words and actions because mommy or daddy did it. Because we say it or do it, it must be ok. Often, that parroting takes place at a most unwanted time.

- How often has a child uttered words he really doesn't understand at the most inappropriate time, words we wouldn't share with, for example, our church family?
- How do our young kids learn sarcasm, the use of snide tones, and body language with verbal outbursts clearly beyond their years?
- We don't actively teach our kids to be racists or bigots, or to know hatred and harsh anger. Yet we see it in them on occasion.

When born, and in their first couple of years, our kids are pure. They don't say or do any of those things. Some of it is learned *in the home* by the time they reach 5 or 6, and by the time they are socializing with other kids, their learning curve increases. That said, it is still at the home where the majority of that "training" takes place. They are like sponges—absorbing little guys.

Bottom Line Thought: What do your kids hear and see from you that can have a negative effect on their relationships present and future? Are your words and actions such that your little sponges will grow to be kind, considerate, loving, humble, caring and godly people?

Day 16:
Our Complaint Meter

Have you recently complained about?

> not getting calls or texts, only to discover that your phone was not turned on or on mute?

> running out of gas in your car only to realize that you had forgotten to fill it?

> getting a dunning notice because you forgot to pay that bill?

> how much your wife has changed even though you have dropped the ball on keeping that marriage alive?

> how wild and ill mannered your kids are, even though the amount of time you have devoted to them has continued to diminish?

> how your boss thinks about you, even though you know you haven't given the job your all?

> your problems and complaints without taking a good look inside yourself?

> your church even though you are not a regular attendee and don't participant in what they offer?

When our complaint meter starts to reach this level, it's in the red zone. This type of complainer will most likely be the one to complain about a silent God, and yet his bible will have a coat of dust on it from lack of use. This complainer will have gotten out of the habit of regularly setting aside time for prayer, time when he shares all with God and then patiently waits for God's direction. This type of complainer is not in community with other men as together they share, love, support, reaffirm, and shepherd each other. Sometimes, this man will call himself a Christian.

Bottom Line Thought: If you complaint meter is starting to red-line, what steps can you take to turn things around? If a friend or associate is like this, how can you help him change?

Day 17:
4 Eyes

I went to grade school in Detroit for a year because of dad's job transfer. It was there that I experienced my first taste of bullying. The kids loved to pick on me for several reasons:

- They were very street-wise, I was anything but,
- I had grown up in Florida and Georgia, and was *very* southern.
- I had a butch haircut; they had slicked back hair.
- and, I wore glasses with thick corrective lenses.

They called me "4-eyes", and I hated it. I couldn't lash out because I was small, and I was chicken. It was one against many which wasn't good. Dad eventually got transferred back to Georgia, Later I had corrective surgery and I no longer needed glasses. Bully issue solved.

What do we see in our minds eye when we see others

- who are a different race than we are?
- who are of a much lower socio-economic status than we are?
- of the opposite sex and are very nice looking?
- who are obviously of a different sexual orientation?
- who we don't like because they are just "different"?
- who seem overly crabby, angry, or negative?
- who are homeless or street beggars?
- who are just plain "weird" in how they dress and mark their bodies?

I am ashamed to say that I see things in those people that God would never see. I can react with lust, anger, disgust, abhorrence, haughtiness, hatred, or bewilderment. In those moments, I have neglected to think that we are <u>all</u> God's children, nothing more, nothing less. I have failed to consider that the crabby, angry, negative person was having a terrible time dealing with some stuff and wasn't handling it well. I have neglected to think of the homeless and street beggars as real people with real needs. The list goes on.

I would love to be called 4-eyes again if it meant that I <u>consistently</u> looked at every situation and person through God's eyes instead of just my own. How different would this world be if all of us set that example for our children?

Bottom Line Thought: How hard will it be to take it one step at a time to see through God's eyes so that you would welcome being called 4-eyes?

Day 18:
Are We Just Saying It?

During the worship part of our church service we sometimes sing a song that never gets old to me. It's a song that makes me do some soul searching. The title of the song is Here's My Heart. Passion is the group that sings it. Here's the chorus:

> Here's my heart, Lord,
> Here's my heart, Lord,
> Here's my heart, Lord,
> Speak what is true.
> Here's my life, Lord,
> Here's my life, Lord,
> Here's my life, Lord,
> Speak what is true,
> Speak what is true.

The message is straightforward and simple, isn't it? When sung, felt, and meant, it forces us to open our hearts and lives to hear what God is saying to us. The song can force us to respond to the chorus by wanting to open our hearts and lives to let Him in to do His work within us. It's at those moments that I find myself not just saying it, but deeply feeling it. It's become a strong Jesus moment to me as evidenced by the emotions I feel as I sing it.

Those are the moments and times we wish we could live *all of the time* while we walk down the narrow dirt road that is our life. It is at those moments that we are fully embracing God and what He wants of us. And it is at those moments when we are not just saying it, we are living it. It is at those times that I experience a moment of heaven here on earth.

When church is over and it's time to spend another 6 days in the "real" world, I remind myself to use the take-away from that time. I can use the take-away throughout the week by praying regularly. I can give Him my heart and life through prayer and ask Him to speak to me. It's all about whether I choose to or not. And, it all depends on whether I'm just saying it or if I am actually doing it.

Bottom Line Thought: Are you just saying it and feeling it on Sundays, or do you try to keep it alive all week?

Day 19:
Easy? Yeah, right.

I recently had one of those days when everything was right, when everything clicked just like it should, and this was without my engineering it. It was one of those not too often days when all was well with all that was around me and within me. I felt blessed to the maximum. My past didn't bother me, nor did anything in the present. I really felt like I was at one with God

Then it happened. It was late in the day and something happened that turned the day inside out. It really wasn't a big deal. What *was* the big deal was the big deal I made out of it. In the span of a few heartbeats I saw all that had made me feel so blessed go flying out of the window. My sense of calm, peace, harmony with God, joy, and the love I had been feeling vanished. I dug inside of me (I didn't have to go too far) and found some anger, attitude, emotions, indignation, and pride to replace what had flown out the window. To make it a perfect scene, I engaged my mouth to stir the pot.

The situation ended only after I had made a complete fool of myself, and I soon discovered that I, and only I, had to own that one. Doing that was no easier than maintaining the earlier feelings of being so blessed.

How did the switch from feeling so God filled to that of being such a broken person happen so quickly?

- I lost focus of what was good and right
- I looked at the situation out of anger, not out of love
- I failed to dig inside of me to use the God tools in my toolbox.
- I allowed the broken parts inside of me dictate my reactions

Later, I was able to resolve the situation by praying, asking forgiveness for those actions, accepting my errors, and offering forgiveness for my actions to the offended party. It was a lesson that at any time and anywhere it may not be easy to control myself and to hold onto those good moments in time.

Bottom Line Thought: Does your broken human side sometimes supersede who God intends you to be? How do you deal with those times?

Day 20:
About That Prayer Thing.

Have you had any of those moments when you thought that if you prayed you would hear God say something like, "Dude, if you're going to be praying to me, don't be praying *like that* to ME," or "come on, man!"? I've had those moments, sad to say. I thought that if I didn't pray a "happy" prayer He might not be interested, or that if I was raw-gut honest about what was really going on He might be disgusted. Things have changed. It took a while in my journey before I was able to put it all together with clarity. It was a DUH experience when it became clear.

- He knows me like a book
- He knows all that I do, think, and feel
- He surrounds me with His love 24/7/365
- He <u>wants</u> to hear me, no matter what is going on
- He will answer, in His time and in His way
- I simply need to be open to hearing Him, trusting Him, and following Him

What makes it easier, and actually more real to pray now, is that I know I can talk to Him just as I would talk to any friend. I don't need fancy words, I don't need somber tones, I don't have to pretend so that my prayer sounds "happy" or "God like", nor do I have to impress anyone with my prayer. All He asks is that I pray. He's told me *"let it rip man, bring it on."* That makes it so less complicated.

Bottom Line Thought: Do you struggle with prayer? Do you sometimes feel you have to be an "un-real" you to be able to pray so-called "properly"? Have you freed yourself to just be the real you when you pray?

Day 21:
5 Simple Truths

Life changing truth situations require that there are 2 participants, a giver and a taker. The giver gives out of love with no expectation of a return. The taker has no expectation that it's going to happen. For both the giver and taker there are no strings attached. It's almost like a random act of kindness thing, but more. These situations will often become the catalyst for a changed life. Here they are:

1. Always leave people better than you found them.
2. Hug the hurt.
3. Kiss the broken.
4. Befriend the lost.
5. Love the lonely.

Gee, that sounds like how Jesus lived and interacted with people in His day. We should consider that as we try to duplicate His walk in our efforts to be more Christ like.

Bottom Line Thought: In your ordinary everyday life do you look for those opportunities where you can duplicate Jesus' walk?

Day 22:
Michael Jordan

Arguably Michael Jordan is the greatest professional basketball player who ever played the game. He is a worldwide recognized icon of the game. It was a thrill to watch him play at the old Chicago Stadium. He could make moves on the court that were all but impossible. There are some things about Jordan, however, that perhaps some are unaware of:

- He missed more than 9 thousand shots in his career.
- He lost almost 300 of the games he played.
- He failed to make the game winning shot 26 times.

Jordan never gave up in spite of his failures, and he succeeded. The failures that we make in our lives offer us the opportunity to succeed as well. The only failure that can possibly take us down is the one we allow to take us down. If we deal with our failures, even those we might consider fatal, with the attitude that we will work through them at all costs, we will succeed. We will always experience some failures.

If we allow our failures to block our journey, we will never become fully devoted followers of Christ. The failures will become our focus, not Him. We need to make each of those failures stepping stones toward our success. The successes we experience will free us in our life as Christian men.

Unlike Jordan, we may not end up selling tennis shoes, but if we draw success out of our failures, our eternal prize, heaven, will always be our greatest success.

Bottom Line Thought: Do you recognize your failures? Have you let them stand in the way of your relationship with the Lord by overpowering you? How can you deal with your failures so that your walk as a Christ follower will be made stronger?

Day 23:
Use Your Imagination

Here's a quick, easy little test for any men who have children who aren't adults yet, or for men who will be fathers. It can also be shared by men whose sons and daughters have children.

Close your eyes and have a quiet moment.

Think only about your young daughter.

Will you want her to date or marry a guy just like you?

Did you smile?

No?

Then start changing.....NOW!

Close your eyes once again and take a quiet moment.

Think only about your young son.

Imagine that he is growing up just like you.

Did you smile?

No?

Then start changing ......NOW!

Day 24:
Follow The Dog

We adopted a dog named Duke. He's an older "gentleman" lab that's perpetually happy. He loves everyone so much that sometimes I worry that he might throw his back out by wagging his tail so hard. He's a joy around both people and other dogs. He assumes the best in them, he's happy and content around them, and it's obvious that he loves them.

I recently had lunch with Norm**, a man from church who "adopted" me as a man who needed mentoring. Norm's full of spiritual wealth that he shares, something I need in my life on a regular basis. He's a living anchor, rudder, and sounding board for me. I mentioned to him that we had baby-sat 3 of our grandsons a few days past so mom and dad could enjoy a rare date night. I mentioned that I felt inadequate as a grandfather, just as I had as a father. I feel stiff and rigid around little kids. It's hard for me to be spontaneously open, happy and silly when around them. I feel like I'm too adult when around children and can't "loosen" up. I shared that it makes me sad and angry at myself when it happens. Norm asked about my role models when I grew up, and I told him there was just one grandfather alive then, and my dad. They were each the same way as I am. He quietly thought that over for a few minutes.

Then he lit up as he made a surprising comment. He animatedly said three words. *"Follow the dog."* Since he knows our dog well, he went on to paint a word picture for me using Duke as the example. He explained how Duke meets kids at their level, something I can do with practice. He suggested that perhaps I unknowingly was thinking that the kids could reach me at my level because of a lack of a role model as a kid. He suggested that I could try to look at the time with my grandkids as a special play time, just as the dog does, and repeated, "Follow the dog."

My take-away from that conversation was this:

- I shouldn't take myself so seriously
- It's ok to be a kid again when with the kids
- I shouldn't bring old baggage to those special times
- Be loose, happy, and feel blessed by them. Special times won't last.
- By my being aware of these things when with them, the kids may cherish those moments more than I may ever know.

Bottom Line Thought: Follow the dog.

** See Epilogue

Day 25:
The Repairman

What if our car or truck breaks and it's beyond our ability to fix it ourselves?

We take it to the repairman.

What do we do when our computer, heater, or refrigerator goes on the fritz and we can't afford a new one?

We call the repairman.

If we fell and broke an arm, or if we got acutely ill all of a sudden, what do we do?

We go see the repairman who is called a doctor

What should we do when we know our heart isn't quite right, or

- We sense that our relationship with God isn't what it should be,
- We are feeling gnawing doubts about Him or ourselves,
- We are struggling with sin that just won't let go,
- Our lives are just upside down and we're out of sorts,
- We feel like just giving up?

We go to the repair <u>MAN</u>.

The head wrench at the garage for humans is God. He may be the one repairman we least feel like seeing at those times. But, what's the alternative? A broken human, just like a car, refrigerator, or arm, can't fix itself. The problem will only become worse. The repairmen for those earthly things have to diagnose and check the problems before they can fix them. Our repairman *already knows* what the problem is, and He knows what the fix is. The fix is us. We begin to fix those problems within us when we decide we need fixing, and we call Him. He's waiting for that call, and He will be immediately available to help us. And, He warranties all of His work.

Bottom Line Thought: Why wouldn't you take all that needs fixing in you to the Head Wrench? Do you really trust how you would fix yourself?

Day 26:
Where Are You Looking?

I remember playing a game when I was a young boy called "Up, Down, Looking all Around." If I recall correctly, it was a version of "Hide and Seek", except it was hidden objects we were looking for instead of kids.

As adults we do a lot of looking up and down, looking all around, more than we realize. If, while traveling, we make a wrong turn and find ourselves in what looks like a nasty neighborhood, we will look around a lot. When we're out in nature and see some beautiful landscapes, mountain ranges, or canyons, we look around to take it all in.

People look around to find the right car to buy, the right home to buy, and even the right girl to marry. We also spend a lot of time looking around to find God don't we? At times, all that looking around effort just gives us uncertain results. How often do we take the time to just be still and

> Look back and thank God,
> Look forward and trust God,
> Look around and serve God,
> Look within and find God?

A good look inward will allow us to completely look back, forward, and around and make some truths clear:

- By looking back and thanking Him, we are able to see just how far He has brought us from the men we were to the men we are.
- As we look forward with trust, we are able to see how many difficult times He has helped us through and know that He will be there for future difficulties.
- As we look around He will reveal the gifts He has entrusted to us and lead us to service opportunities for His Kingdom work.
- As we look within, it becomes clear how He has always been with us, no matter what, and that He always will be.

Bottom Line Thought: Are you just looking around, or are you *really* looking? Are you looking in the right place?

Day 27:
Stones And Glass Houses

I had a window cleaning business for a few years and one of my customers lived in a town known for the wealth of the residents and their enormous fancy homes. Twice a year my customer would call me to clean the mirrors in their very large master bath. What made the job, not only difficult, but unique, was that *every single surface* of the bathroom, with the exception of the fixtures and the counter top was mirrored. One of the tradesmen more familiar with the family told me once that the bathroom itself had cost over seventy five thousand dollars. Needless to say, I'm sure that nothing ever got thrown in that bathroom.

"Don't throw stones if you live in a glass house" is a phrase that's been around a long time. There are many variations of what the term means. One is that we shouldn't insult, hurt, or judge others by our words or actions because they could easily do the same to us. The intent closely follows a biblical saying we often hear, "do unto others as we would do unto ourselves." Those sayings warn us that since we aren't perfect or without flaws, we are no better than anyone else, and we should treat them like we want to be treated. Yet, don't we throw insults or judge others because it somehow makes us feel superior to them in some way?

Perhaps we need to think of ourselves as living in glass houses. Wouldn't it be easier for us to relate to others in a more God like manner if we did? Because many of us aren't very transparent with others, it might help us to see more about ourselves, and our stuff, the stuff we don't want to see.

> WHILE YOU
> WERE BUSY
> JUDGING OTHERS
> YOU LEFT YOUR
> CLOSET OPEN AND
> YOUR SKELETONS
> FELL OUT.

We all have our skeletons, just as we all have our faults. When we sling those insults and judge others, the only thing it accomplishes is that it allows others to see right through our glass houses so they can see who, and what, we really are.

Bottom Line Thought: Picking up glass isn't fun. Do you throw stones at others while living in your glass house?

Day 28:
What If?

What would you think if you received this letter from your wife and kids?

Dear (your name):

Sometimes your words or actions tell us that you think we need a nicer car just because you want one. It's the same when you talk about a bigger, fancier house, or a really "wow" vacation, or the flashiest gifts for birthdays and Christmas. It sometimes feels like bigger and better stuff, and expensive toys like the latest electronics, boats, and other things are somehow going to make our lives more satisfying and fulfilled. Is this what you are really thinking?

(Your name), here's what really matters to us. The single most important thing you can do is to work hard at being the spiritual leader of this family. We don't need new fancy cars or any of that other stuff if it means that you will have to work more and harder, and be away from us more because that's what it takes to get those things. That is especially true if it would mean that your main role, being the spiritual leader, would suffer.

All we really want, (your name), is your time and your heart. That is so much more important than things and stuff. You have no idea how we love your smile, your wit, your honesty, your openness, and your effort. As long as we are your true priority, that is all that matters. We are forever. Things and stuff may not be.

(Your name), we love you just as you are, and we are happy with everything we have. Being just you impresses us much more than any stuff you think we may like. Let's keep it simple and keep our focus on who we are—a family, and not what we sometimes feel we need to be—people with a lot of stuff we don't really need to have

We love you.

It's real easy to succumb to the Monster of More isn't it? Sometimes it's hard not to want to keep up with the mythical Jones's, and we fall into that trap more than is good for us. Bigger and better isn't necessarily best.

Bottom Line Thought: Financially comfortable or not, sometimes we all think bigger and better is best. Would a letter like this get your attention? What can you change so you don't get a letter like this one?

Day 29:
Sliced Bread

Have you heard the phrase "that's better than sliced bread"? We use the term when we are amazed about something new to us, or something unique that does a job—like a tool specially made for one purpose, one that replaces one that was not just right for the job prior to that. Perhaps when color TV's came out to replace the old black and whites the saying was used in many households.

Why don't we start this day off as a better than sliced bread day? Let's make it a real "up" day! Just like everyone else on God's green earth, we have our issues, our problems, our baggage and hurts. We have our uncertainties and our struggles to face as we walk yet another day in this walk of life. But, we certainly don't have to be down about it because we *can* all choose to be proud of ourselves for *something*.

Let's start this day as an "I'm better than sliced bread" day—because we are just that today. We are free to be us, we know that God shares His unconditional love with us, and we realize that we aren't the men we used to be. We have purpose, and we know we are not alone in our journey—no matter how rough it might be.

Bottom Line Thought: Repeat after me—"I am better than sliced bread today." Now, go enjoy your day in a happy mode!

Day 30:
I Hate That

What is hate? It means to feel hostility toward, to detest. I don't like the word "hate" because it's a hateful word. It's a negative term that describes, in an over the top way, a passion filled dislike for something or someone. That said, for quite some time in my life, hate was, indeed, a part of my life and mindset:

1. I grew up in Florida and Georgia in the '50's and early '60's. In the culture I grew up in racial hatred was the norm. Blacks weren't black then. They were referred to by another name, seldom heard today. I hated blacks because that is all I was exposed to.
2. I also came to hate homosexuals (they weren't called gays then). Not only was it a part of the culture I grew up in to hate them, as a naïve youngster there were several incidents where I was taken advantage of by some homosexuals which scared my life for a long time.

My obvious and visible hatred of both of those parts of our society lasted well into adulthood. There were many layers of onion skin to pull back to get rid of it to free me to start accepting all people as simply members of the human race. In the second example it took years to learn to love the sinner and hate the sin. To grow, I had to let go of many ingrained and developed generalizations and assumptions I held about people. I had to let go of my hate.

Life is like monkey bars. You have to let go if you want to move on.

Bottom Line Thought: Are there things in your life that are holding you back from spiritual growth? If you labeled each bar on the monkey bar set with those things you need let go of that are interfering with your growth as a man, what would they be?

Day 31:
Thin Slicing

Have you heard of "thin slicing?"
"Thin Slicing"--zeroing in on the cultural, racial, economic, appearance, educational, social, physical, and physical differences in those with whom we come in contact, and categorizing them to see how they stack up to our perception <u>of ourselves</u>. It's like profiling, but worse. In other words, we judge others by our own *assumptions*, which may be false. For example, a black, gay, handicapped and deformed, street person with little education would be a disgusting object on the sidewalk to many of us passing by. That's a graphic example. Most of the thin slicing we do in our daily lives is much more subtle than that. Further, the habit is a result of our human, almost inborn, need to thin slice when dealing with people.

What does thin slicing do to us? We get spiritual hernias from it by carrying all the extra weight it creates. The weight comes from the sheer volume of judging which we do. Perhaps this will help explain it. Having grown up with so many false assumptions about blacks, Hispanics, and homosexuals, I went through years of automatically thin slicing those groups. As a result I was spiritually weighed down because my focus was on anything but their hearts and their conditions. I carried their "weaknesses" and "faults" in an unhealthy context, with no understanding that with each passing day my heart was becoming harder, and heavier. With that kind of thin slicing there is no room for unity, compassion, learning, forgiveness, or love. The heart becomes heavy, and a spiritual hernia is the result.

God does not, nor has He ever, thin sliced, because He loves us all equally and unconditionally. Jesus, during His time on earth never thin sliced--in fact, just the opposite. He sought out those who we would thin slice at first glance.

Bottom Line Thought: Do you thin slice and perhaps not realize it?

- Do you thin slice the kids your kids play with?
- Do you do it with associates, customers, clients, and folks you meet through your job?
- Do you do it with folks who visit your church the first time?

Day 32:
Troubled Sleep

A true story

It seemed as if he had lain in bed for hours, restless, trying to get to sleep because he was tired. Try as he might, he couldn't get near that wonderful zone of body and mind relaxation that comes right before sleep. It wasn't that he was overwhelmed with any particular thing. It was simply that his mind was unusually restless, panning over any number of insignificant things, never pausing long enough to do any real thinking about any of it. He was just restless and out of sorts.

The thought of music zipped through his mind as a part of the disconnect symphony that was playing there. He thought music sooths and calms. As he had done on other nights when he had just wanted the sheer joy of listening to some soft Christian music playing quietly, he decided he would listen to his I-pod. So, out of the warm bed he went in search of it. As he made his way back to bed he started to think, jokingly, that the sounds of Christian and Gospel music would be just the exorcism he needed to drive his body to the sleep he wanted. Once back in bed with the ear buds in, he realized that with the music streaming through them that sleep wasn't going to happen. But, what did occur was even better. Calmness came over his heart and mind. His body started to react to the music in the most common of ways. Finger tapping, feet jiggling, and finally hands raising as the praise and worship songs played.

As the music cycled through, something started to stir in his heart, and with that some clarity of thought struck his mind. It was as if he was totally isolated from all that is earthly, amazingly so. He clearly saw himself as he *really* was. He was a broken man, a man so prone to sin and to neglecting God's will for him, a man consumed with his need to control, a man who was scared because he felt that he just couldn't "get it right." And in that moment of clarity he also saw God's hand extended toward him, and he could almost feel the breath that came from the voice that said to him "I've got you man, I've got you. You're mine. We can do this."

The ear buds came out in an instant. The tears that had started to fall were wiped away from his eyes as his knees hit the floor alongside the bed. The house was completely silent except for the voice of the man kneeling as he started to pray. "Fix me Father; fix all that is wrong in my heart. Heal me Father, and let me bask in the glow of the scars from that healing. Take me Father, do whatever it is that you want with me, and lead me there as you make me willing to follow. Make me willing to be built into the man that you want me to be, to do whatever it is, wherever it is, and whenever it is, that you want. Take my heart and wrap it in the protection of your hands to protect me from me. Do all this so that together we can fight the demons that plague me so much. And he cried, and cried.

Spent, he crawled back in bed. And sleep came quickly as he felt that he was there with the arms of Jesus wrapped around him. It was a quiet sleep, a peaceful sleep, a calm sleep.

Bottom Line Thought: Have you ever freed your heart and emotions so much that you felt you were in close communion with God? Were you able to sense, with full certainty, that it was just your heart and Him openly and deeply sharing and loving?

Day 33:

Grasp His Hand

K-LOVE is a Christian radio station. It also shares a lot of encouragement through stories and guest appearances. A while back a young man shared his story in an interview with the radio staff. He had been a heavy meth user. Meth is very addictive, and it can mess a person up. It's a hard addiction to overcome. The young man related that he had been "kind of messed up" on a sidewalk when two young men about his age, came up to him and with little conversation, invited him to go to church with them. It was right out of the blue. It wasn't sidewalk preaching, they simply asked if he would to go to church with them. To his own surprise, he agreed to go.

In the interview he told how he had gone with them, and while at the service he strongly felt the need to accept Christ and get off of the meth. He did just that. The interview, by the way, was about 15 months after he had gone to the church with those strangers, and he was still a Christ follower, still clean, with no relapses along the way.

One of the interviewers asked him, "Looking back, what do you take out of that experience"? The young man's response was simple and powerful. He said, "Jesus is always walking right along with you. All you have to do is grasp His hand." That statement should speak to all of us. It's likely we all intellectually know it, but it's equally likely that we don't always practice it on a regular basis.

How often, when we are we experiencing life's bumps and grinds, do we grasp His hand and feel secure knowing that He will lead us through whatever it is we are going through, no matter what it is? Sometimes we just forget about that hand extended toward us, the one we need to grasp.

That hand--it's always there.
If only we would care
to grasp that hand of love,
that hand from up above.

Joe Miller, 2015

Bottom Line Thought: Are you going through life with just your own 2 hands? Why?

Day 34:
Unhappy?

There's a saying that goes something like this-- "when momma ain't happy, ain't no one happy." The meaning is simple and applies to us all. When we're not happy, those around us may not be. They will be on edge, cautious about what they say and do and they may be ill at ease being around us. We're all going to have unhappy times, but what matters is if we have grown into a consistent state of unhappiness. It is then that our relationships will suffer.

7 qualities of a chronically unhappy man

1. *His default belief is that life is hard.* Yes, life is hard, but a happy man doesn't roll over and play victim to it. He will fight through the hard times and persevere.
2. *He thinks that most people cannot be trusted.* It is healthy to be cautious in new relationships, but not to the point of not being able to see others hearts and foster a sense of community.
3. *He focuses on what is wrong, not what is right.* There are many wrongs in the world, but we can't turn a blind eye to what's right and dwell on the wrongs. The happy man knows there are wrongs, and balances the wrongs with the rights.
4. *He strives to control his life.* He micromanages his life to control the outcomes and is upset when things go wrong. A happy man uses his energy to reach goals, and knows he can't control the curve balls that occur.
5. *He compares himself to others and harbors jealousy.* His focus is on the good fortune of others and his lack of it. A happy man believes in unlimited possibilities and embraces the good fortune of others.
6. *He looks at his future with worry and fear.* He looks at what can go wrong. A happy man will daydream about how he hopes life will unfold for him, and knows that God will guide all of his steps.
7. *He tends to gossip and complain unrealistically.* They live in their past mistakes and failures, and will gossip about others. The happy man lives in the here and now and thinks forward.

Men who are striving to be Christ followers will be unhappy at times because there are times when it is right and appropriate.

Bottom Line Though: Are the 7 traits of unhappiness affecting your relationship with others and God?

Day 35:
Gifts

We like gifts don't we? Yes, I know we don't like the gifts of sweaters that we would never choose for ourselves, or the shirts that don't fit like we would prefer. This is about real gifts, gifts which we are grateful for. There's an "ism" about real gifts: *if you don't recognize it, you can't be grateful for it.* Here are 4 characteristics of real gifts:

1. A real gift comes from a giver.
2. A real gift costs something to give.
3. Giving real gifts is a gamble.
4. Real gifts take us by surprise.

What does that mean as we go through our everyday lives striving to be better men? Let's look at it through our spiritual glasses. God, the giver, sent His son (a real gift) freely (it cost us nothing to receive Him), to save us (a gamble since He knew some would reject it). If we are men who accepted that gift, aren't we amazed at how that real gift took us from where we were to where we are now? I am. If that's the case, aren't we overwhelmingly grateful? I am. There's a big take-away we can grab from this and apply to our everyday lives:

Relentlessly look for gifts,
Relentlessly pursue gratitude.

In grasping that take-away, we will all be amazed at the multitude of little gifts that come our way each day, and our sense of gratitude will strengthen and grow. The little things will become more important to us. We should also realize that a deeper sense of humility will foster a depth of gratitude we haven't experienced before.

Bottom Line Thought: Are you too focused on the big things to appreciate the little things that come your way? What might be standing in your way of experiencing more gratitude?

Day 36:
None But Us

There are many things that can happen that will impact our lives in some way, for good or for bad. They will help us or hurt us on our journey toward becoming better men. There is one single event that happened over two thousand years ago that affects us all. That was when God sent His son to die on the cross for us.

That event paved the way to a huge obligation we now have. Many have taken on that obligation; some have failed to grasp it. Through His death, Jesus was no longer here to carry out His father's work. That was the plan. Prior to Him dying on the cross, Jesus prepared 12 others, known as the Apostles, to go out into the world (our world) and make disciples. By doing so, they were doing Kingdom work.

Our obligation, should we choose, is no different than what Jesus prepared His 12 Apostles to do, and that is, do Kingdom work. If we accept that it all started all those many years ago, there is no question how it is done today—person to person, man to man. Mother Theresa made it quite clear in this saying attributed to her:

"Christ has no body on earth but yours, no hands but yours, no feet but yours. Yours are the eyes through which Christ's compassion for the world is to look out; yours are the feet with which He is to go about doing good, and yours are the hands with which He is to bless us now."

Jesus (the live Jesus) is long gone. So are the Apostles. So are the disciples they made, and the disciples they made, and right on through the passage of time to us. There's nobody left but us. It is us who are in the here and now. We have been entrusted to practice discipleship as followers of Christ.

Bottom Line Thought: Are you using your body, hands, feet, eyes, and heart to do what you have been entrusted to do?

Day 37:
Burning Embers

This, from an unknown source, speaks volumes about our hot and cold spiritual selves:

"A member of a church, who had previously been attending services regularly, stopped going. After a period of time the pastor decided to visit him. It was a chilly evening. The pastor found the man at home alone, sitting before a blazing fire in the fireplace. Guessing the reason for the pastor's visit, the man welcomed him, led him to a comfortable chair near the fireplace and waited.

The pastor made himself at home, but said nothing. After some moments, the pastor took the fire tongs, carefully picked up a brightly burning ember and placed it to one side of the hearth all alone. Then he sat back in his chair, still silent.

The host watched all this in quiet contemplation. As the one lone ember's flame flickered and diminished, there was a momentary glow and then its fire was no more. Soon it was cold and dead. Not a word had been spoken since the initial greeting. The pastor looked at his watch and realized that it was time to leave. He slowly stood up, picked up the cold dead ember, and placed it back in the middle of the fire. Immediately it began to glow once more from the light and heat from the coals around it.

As the pastor reached the door to leave, his host said with a tear running down his cheek, 'thank you so much, and especially for your fiery message. I will be back in church next Sunday.' They shook hands as the pastor left."

We live in a world today when people sometimes try to say too much, when just a little would do. As a result, some won't listen. Sometimes the best messages are the ones left unspoken.

Bottom Line Thought: When you feel your spiritual fire dying, what can you do to let that light shine once again? Are you free to share your burning embers with someone whose may be dying?

Day 38:
Indian Lore

Native American Indian culture is interesting to many people. Wildly different than what we experienced from the early cowboys and Indians shows, there are things about the true Indian culture that are fascinating. The culture has always had a way of mingling nature, its laws, and the animal kingdom with their own sense of spirituality. Out of that has come Indian lore, really much of it is wisdom, which has been passed on from generation to generation. One piece of that lore from an unknown source follows:

> An old Cherokee told his grandson, "My son, there is a battle between two wolves inside us all. One is Evil. It is anger, jealousy, greed, resentment, inferiority, lies, and ego. The other is Good. It is joy, peace, love, hope, humility, kindness, empathy, and truth."
>
> The boy thought about it and asked, "Grandfather, which one wins?"
>
> The old man quietly replied, "The one you feed."

I don't know if that is an actual piece of Indian lore or not. I do understand the message it shares with us. I see a bit of me in that example, as I think most of us would. Sometimes it feels like there are those two wolves circling around in my heart and mind just waiting to fight. And sometimes they do! That's called spiritual warfare.

I know a couple of things about the wolves in my life. Neither one will completely die if I don't feed them. They will go dormant, but won't die. And I know one thing for certain. The one I choose to feed will absolutely grow stronger.

Bottom Line Thought: Which wolf are you feeding most of the time?

Day 39:
God's Top 10 List

Most of us have heard of David Letterman. He periodically puts David Letterman's Top 10 List of something on his show. They are usually pretty funny, quite pointed, often sarcastic, but always well delivered, as only he can do. We hear them, we laugh at them, and then we generally forget them.

Did you know that God has His own top 10 list? No, I'm not referring to the Ten Commandments. Those are rules to live by. His top 10 list are things we can remember to help us through the peaks and valleys and the rough spots of our spiritual journey. They can see us through our day, every day.

10 Things God Wants Us to Remember

> I will give you rest.
>
> I will strengthen you.
>
> I will answer you.
>
> I believe in you.
>
> I will bless you.
>
> I will not fail you.
>
> I am for you.
>
> I will provide for you.
>
> I will remain with you.
>
> I love you unconditionally.

There is nothing funny or sarcastic about that list. It is very simple, pointed, direct, and very well delivered all throughout the Word. His list is something we can all live by if we have the faith to believe it. That is a choice He also gives us to make.

Bottom Line Thought: Letterman's lists, or God's list?

Day 40:
The Brain Shelf

I visited a friend a while back and it wasn't a pleasant visit. In the conversation he kept revisiting things that had happened to him in the past. He spoke like he couldn't let it go. He seemed angry and upset. He knew there was nothing he could do about it and was puzzled why he couldn't drop it.

I shared that we all have good junk and bad junk (such as his) floating in our heads. It's like to space junk. It's there, and we can't get rid of it. It's because we have memories, though sometimes dormant, of all of the good and bad experiences in our lives, and our memories retain it. I went on that when our lives are changed because we became Christians, we tend to make more of it than we used to because we are looking at it from a different spiritual view, and it bothers us.

I shared how I deal with my junk. I compartmentalize it. I have mentally built 2 closets in my mind, each with shelves. One closet is for good junk, the other for bad junk. I boxed up the good junk and the bad junk and put the boxes on shelves in their respective closets. Hey, the stuff is always going to be there, it will go to the grave with me, so why not try to make it orderly!

Now when some of that bad junk starts bothering me I can react differently. I simply acknowledge that one of the boxes fell off its shelf, opened up and spilled its contents. All I have to do, instead of massaging it and moaning about it, is tell myself to box it up and put it back on the shelf and close the door.

Through that process, I have learned that the more I take good care of my spiritual condition, the harder it is for the bad junk closet door to open. Yes, it can still open, and it always will. But, it doesn't open as much. It's the evil one who opens it and spills the boxes. He doesn't want me to be happy and content. He wants me in an angry and confused state because then he can manipulate me better.

Bottom Line Thought: Does your bad junk pester you? How do you handle that?

Day 41:
Thanks Man!

"God is great. God is good. And we thank Him for our food."
"Now I lay me down to sleep. I pray the Lord my soul to keep"

Those are simple prayers that many of us learned as kids. They may have been the first prayers we said. I enjoy hearing little kids saying those prayers. They are so sweet and innocent, and oh-so fervent, serious, and full of love. It sounds the same when they nestle up to us parents and say I love you.

Let's think about prayer for just a minute. Not corporate or family prayer. Not bed time prayers. Let's think about spontaneous prayers, those that come to mind at anything but "normal" times. For example:

- like when we're chilling on the back deck enjoying the quiet that came at the end of a great day.
- when we're tooling down the road minding our own business with nothing bothersome on our mind.
- when we just experienced a rush of natural beauty, and are blown away.
- when we heard some wonderfully positive news of a dear one who is ill.

Do we have to wait until a pre-set prayer time to pray about those things? Of course not! Unfortunately some of us do. By waiting we open ourselves for forgetfulness, or we just think "well, it was nice, but."

Abba, our Father, God, won't mind if we spontaneously let a prayer go. It will be so meaningful to Him if he heard an out of the blue heartfelt prayer, one of pure joy or emotion once in a while. Something like "thanks, man, for letting me see that", or, "Dude, that was awesome, I am overwhelmed", or, "God, that was crazy good!" After all, aren't there times when we just want to jump up pointing to the sky and say "I know that was You-- thank you God?"

I think we need to bring that little kid in us back out. We need times when we can be simple, innocent, spontaneous, and uncluttered by ritualistic gotta-dos. So, tell me again what might be wrong with a simple "thank you Man" when there is nobody to get offended or mad."

Bottom Line Thought: Do you ever get urges to have a brief, quick, unorthodox prayer with God? Are you too rigid to try?

Day 42:
The Big Boy Pants

Joe and Shawn, each retired, work together when either of them picks up a job. They need the work to help make ends meet. Each has a checkered past and made a lot of poor decisions while still in their prime working years when they were still healthy. They each now have medical issues that prevent them from working as they once did, and each works through pain on every job they do.

Neither guy whines about either his current situation or the pain he deals with. Both have become believers, and feel very committed to their spiritual growth. Each sees his ugly past as a gift, because each lived through it while others didn't live though a similar past. They look at their individual junk as a positive, because they know God never abandoned them when they made the bad choices that got them to where they are today. He simply waited patiently for the time when they would make the decision that would lead them to being a Christ follower, and He welcomed them and showered each with His grace and redemption.

So now they work happily, without complaint. They are thankful for each job and accept each as a gift. Either guy could, if he so chose, to find any number of things to complain about. But, they don't. Either could, if he so chose, play the game of "should've,-would've,-could've", or sing the "if-only" blues. But, they don't. They are simply thankful that they have the opportunity to do something. And, each happily wears his big boy pants.

Big boy pants are for guys who refuse to dwell on their negatives, their failures, their mistakes or their loss of something they may never have had anyway. Big boy pants aren't for moaners, whiners, or crybabies. Big boy pants are for real men, men who are sure of their relationships, and especially sure of their relationship with God.

Bottom Line Thought: When you get up in the morning, do you put your big boy pants on or are you wearing onesies?

Day 43:
Obituary-itis.

For as long as I can remember, I have had a first thing in the morning routine. My family knows the routine well. I think my routine must have come as part of my habit DNA. One thing about it is that no one should mess with it—it's pretty rigid. Many men may have the same routine. I get up, make the bathroom call, make my coffee, get the paper, and read the paper with my coffee. I am convinced that the paper makes my coffee taste better!

There is a sub-routine that I follow as well. I *must* read the paper in a certain order:

1. The news section
2. The sports section
3. The obituaries.

Following that sub-routine has shown that I have obituary-itis. Obviously, I am always thrilled to see that my name is not in there. I celebrate by getting a 2nd cup of coffee. My day has started off right. However, from reading the obituaries I almost always finding myself coming away from it with some thoughts:

- I find myself happy that I have been allowed to stand another day, that I have one more opportunity to try to be a better man.
- I find myself thankful that God has allowed me to walk this walk of life for as long as He has, and that He has shared so many precious moments with me.
- I also feel a sense of sorrow as I ponder those listed there. I hope that all there had reached unity with our God, and thus were not eternally lost.

Just being alive each day should be enough incentive for each of us to focus on ourselves, our real purpose for being, how we can be an instrument of God's hand in all we do that day, and that our faith and trust in Him will be strong. Perhaps obituary-itis isn't a bad thing.

Bottom Line Thought: If you read the obituaries are your thoughts limited to "boy, am I lucky?" Or, do they help you think of deeper, more spiritual things?

Day 44:
The Right Man

A young man once asked his father, "Father, how will I ever find the right woman?" His father replied, "Forget about finding the right woman, focus on being the right man." That's some awfully sound advice and wisdom isn't it? It's the kind of wisdom I wish I could have shared with my sons as they were growing up.

That little story begs a question doesn't it? What is the right man? Here are some thoughts to answer that question. The right man:

- Wants to be more Christ-like every breathing day.
- Knows he has broken areas and weaknesses and accepts them.
- Continues to work on his broken areas and weaknesses.
- Is humble; he holds his ego in check.
- Embraces his responsibility in every area of his life.
- Sees the good in others and doesn't dwell on their faults.
- Willingly shares of himself and what he has.
- Views women for what they are, not as objects.
- Has unfailing faith and trusts God.

A man who has those qualities is the man that the woman in his life will respect, love and honor. Relationships with those qualities as cornerstones will withstand the test of time, the pressures, and the surprises of everyday life that comes with marriage. They are the glue that holds marriages together when the storms of life come as they always do. They are God honoring to the fullest extent.

Bottom Line Thought: Whether single or married, do you work on these qualities in yourself so that you can be more God honoring?

Day 45:
Attaboy

We all know what an attaboy is, right? It's the same as saying "good job" or "well done." It's really "that a boy" made to sound quirky, because we give attaboys, as in you'll get an attaboy for that. It sounds better than you'll get a "good job" for that one.

As men walking through our lives in the change mode we have chosen, we get lots of advice, opinions, and messages from friends, mentors, books, the Bible, pastors, etc. We do a lot of thinking about ourselves and our journey, so much so that sometimes we think we're on overload. That's part of the process that happens when we start to think, "The more I know, the more I know I need to know". That's natural, especially since we all have those necessary obligations we need just to do life—jobs, families, and down time.

With that, we might feel a bit of frustration with ourselves. When that happens, we tend to start beating ourselves up with such thoughts as "I'm not doing good enough", or "why can't I just get it?" or "is this how it is with other guys?" If, or when, we start thinking that way, it's time to take a break. No, not a break from all we are doing! It's time to get selfish for a minute. It's time to give ourselves an attaboy.

In our journey we don't get many attaboys. We get encouragement when others in our circle see us struggling, but spontaneous attaboys aren't very common. It's as if the change we are seeking is expected, something we need or ought to do. Often lost in the shuffle is the fact that we made a deliberate choice to change ourselves to be men of God.

So we shouldn't expect, or look for, attaboys. That's a selfish privilege we should reserve for ourselves. It's one we should use more often. It's good to look back at our walk to see our progress and victories. It's healthy to quietly acknowledge how far we've come, and it's perfectly fine to humbly give ourselves a great big attaboy. And, while we're giving ourselves an attaboy for making and sticking with it, we must give an attaboy to the one who has walked right alongside us, God.

Bottom Line Thought: Have you taken the time to give yourself an attaboy recently?

Day 46:
First Class Mail

A while back I was going through an old Bible I no longer use and I came across a letter I received 20 years ago. It was hand written (who uses cursive now?) and the paper it was on was yellowed and a bit worn. I read the letter. It was deeply personal, and it went into great detail about the relationship between the writer and me. It painted a clear and transparent word picture of me as I was back then. It was first class mail.

At the time the letter was written, I was a small group leader at the church I was attending. It was a small group that was unusual, and had "just happened." The group consisted of men who were, or had been, total bust-outs. There was not one man in the group who hadn't been a street person, a hard core druggie, an alcoholic, had a jail or prison record, or was an abuser. It was a hard core group of men who had found Jesus the hard way.

The first class mail I mentioned above was part of an exercise our group of grateful, yet broken men, had done. During one of our periodic retreat weekends, one of the exercises we did was to go off by ourselves and think quietly about what Jesus would say to us right then. Then, being open and honest, and totally free, we were to handwrite a letter to ourselves as if it were written by Jesus. It was to be a letter in which Jesus was sharing such things as what He was seeing in us now, how He felt about us, what He wanted of us, what He thought of us, etc. It was a letter that would not be shared in the group, so it could be as real as possible.

As I sat and read the letter "to Joe from Jesus" of 20 years ago, it provided a great snapshot of the man I was then. It also made me wonder what one of those Dear Joe letters would say today if I got the first class mail.

Bottom Line Thought: Most of us pray. Many of us journal, and/or confide in our Christian brothers about what is going on in our lives, what we are thinking. What, if you wrote one, would a letter from Jesus to you say?

Day 47:
Smokey Robinson

In 1967 Smokey Robinson and the Miracles had a hit song called, *I'll Second that Emotion*. The overall message of the song was that the anonymous guy didn't want a kiss and run relationship. Every song has what is called the hook. It's the hook of a song that gets everyone's attention, and makes the song a hit. In Robinson's song, the hook was this:

> *"....if you want*
> *a lifetime of devotion...*
> *I'll second that emotion."*

Folks familiar with the song could hear that short group of words with the music, and they would immediately know what the song was, and probably who sang it. Hooks are what make songs memorable.

Throughout our journey as men looking for ways to be better men, we are exposed to all kinds of things. We do church and hear the messages. We read the Bible and participate in small groups or men's groups. We read books, articles, and papers, and maybe we listen to a Christian radio station. We take what we need for ourselves from those sources, and apply it to our own situation. There's a hook throughout those sources. It's that God loves us. Tha's a powerful and memorable hook.

God has forever been fully devoted to us as His people. My history proves without any doubt that His love for me has never wavered. When there was any wavering done, it was me who did it. Nothing I did could stand in the way of His devotion to me, and the same applies to all of us.

God is like a good parent. He simply wants what is best for us. All He asks of us is a lifetime of devotion to Him.

I'll second that emotion.

Bottom Line Thought: Do you need to simplify things, and get back to basics for a bit, so you can feel that lifetime of devotion He has had for you through all you have done, and all you have been?

Day 48:
Identity Theft

The internet, with its availability, has created a whole new industry within an industry. It's called Identity Theft. It's a big deal that costs folks billions of dollars a year. A case of Identity Theft can ruin a person until they get the case resolved and clean up all the debris left behind which is sometimes no easy task. And even though there is a glut of information out there about how to protect ourselves, often that goes unheeded and some will still get hacked and have their identity used for criminal means.

When we have chosen to be Christ followers, we are identified as Christian men. There are qualities and characteristics that identify us as such. It is those qualities and characteristics that can be attacked and diminished by sin and things of the world which results in the theft of our identity as Christ followers. It's spiritual Identity Theft.

Some of the things which can steal our spiritual identity are:

- Peer pressure
- Laziness or apathy
- A relaxed view of sexual freedoms, and the sanctity of marriage
- A "need to succeed at all costs" mindset
- A "me first" attitude around others
- A lack of humility and the need for control
- Sin in our live that we ignore
- A lack of transparency

We were all created in God's image. As Christian men, we hold as our goal to be more Christ-like. We are working for the prize, heaven. If we are to reach that prize, we need to hold on tightly to those qualities and characteristics that identify us as Christians. Quite simply:

Spiritual goals=spiritual identity.
Earthly goals=identity theft.

Bottom Line Thought: Is your guard up against both types of Identity Theft?

Day 49:
Good Theater

I enjoy an evening out to go see a play at one of the local theaters. I like it because the actors aren't well known, big time actors. They're just ordinary everyday folks like you and I who happen to have the gift and talent to act. They have fun doing it. To me, that's good theater.

In ways, life is like a stage play. Our stage is the world around us. Our audience is all who we come in contact with. Each of us has a story line, just as each of us has a role to play. Each role is different. There are no understudy's, because our story line and role is unique to each of us. The title of our stage play is *Life as a Christian Man*. We each have the lead role because they are one act plays. There is no curtain call after the act is finished. Throughout the whole act there are no actors allowed--only real men.

In life as we do it, we do a lot of play acting. One that jumps right out at me is acting like someone I'm not. Sometimes I really don't want others around me to see me as I really am at that moment in time. So, I'll act. I don't want folks to see me when I'm hurting inside, so I'll do the "I'm fine" act. Or, when there is something really wrong inside of me, I'll glibly give out the old "oh, it's nothing" when asked what's wrong. I think many of us have learned to act those things out in great style.

Then there's that matter of our spiritual condition and how much acting goes on there. How sincere and consistent are we in our efforts to be Christ followers? I'm sure we all know that every play has a stage manager, just like this one act play that we are in. His name is God. He keeps reminding us that this isn't acting. It's more—it's real men playing out their roles in life. All we have to do is follow our lines as we continue to learn our way into heaven. Now that's good theater.

Bottom Line Thought: The one act play that you are in is for nobody's entertainment. It's your life! Are you secure in your role as the lead character?

Day 50:
Bridges And Barriers

Bridges are strong, well planned, and built to last decades. Their purpose is to allow free flowing forward movement. Barriers are easily erected, and have the purpose of stopping or re-directing movement. They cause delays, create anxiety because the route has changed, and disrupt normal traffic movement.

We hear about bridges and barriers when relationships are the topic of conversation. A term such as "building bridges" or "putting up barriers" is commonplace. That is especially true when it come to race relations.

In our own relationships, including our relationship with God, don't we sometimes build bridges or set up barriers? Here are some thoughts about that:

- It is easier to put up a barrier than take the time and effort needed to build a bridge.
- Relationships suffer unnecessarily because of those barriers.
- Bridges can be built or barriers erected at any time and with anyone.
- Barriers don't have to be a permanent blockage in a relationship. They can be removed.

There are some things about bridges and barriers that are important for a Christian man on his spiritual journey to know:

- Committed Christ followers will always try to be *Bridge Builders* who place more emphasis and value on others than themselves.
  - They are dedicated to creating an atmosphere of love and trust in their relationship.
  - They sincerely apologize when they find they have wronged another.
  - They are quick to forgive.
  - They are transparent in their relationships.
  - They are dependable, brutally honest and humble.
- *Barrier Builders* are more interested in themselves than others.
  - While they appear sincere and kind to others, what is going on in the home may be quite different than what is seen.
  - Their worldview is more self-centered.
  - Apologies are difficult, as is forgiveness.
  - They tend to be guarded in what they say and to whom they say it.

Bottom Line Thought: Which are you-- a bridge builder or a barrier builder?

Day 51:
Who Needs A Flashlight When...

There is someone, not a family member, in each of our lives who is special. We admire them immensely and we automatically trust them explicitly because our gut tells us they are special. Almost always they are very, very humble quiet people. They are great listeners, and when they speak their words are filled with loving wisdom. If we were asked who we would most like to be like, our answer would be immediate as we speak their name. They are, in my experience, always genuine Christians.

In my lifetime there have been but two "I would love to be likes". One was Uncle Charlie (not an uncle, but called that) and his wife who befriended our family. He was beyond an inspiration for me in my high school years. In the past few years there has been Norm, my mentor**. Each stood solidly on the rock of Christian principles and never wavered, and both were real men. Their light shined brightly, though neither was in the spotlight.

We all have a yearning to be in the spotlight at times don't we? Our human nature is to want to be the spotlight. To be perfectly blunt about it, aren't there times we delight in tooting our own horns? It's hard not to. That's because we have difficulty with humility.

To some people, humility seems to come naturally. To others, like me, it takes work--a lot of work. The one thing I've seen in people like Uncle Charlie and Norm that explains their humility is that they both are comfortable in their own skin. That's to say they know themselves well, they are on firm ground with their spiritual walk, and their past doesn't control their lives. That frees them to love others like they love themselves. They are not like flashlights which have to be turned or off for the light to shine. Their light is permanently on and it shines as an example to all around them. They don't show their light, they just let it shine, just like Jesus did.

Bottom Line Thought: Do you think anyone might be looking at you as the man they would like to be like? Do you just let your light shine, or do you shine it?

**See Epilogue

Day 52:
Quirks

Quirks are idiosyncrasies. We all have them. One of mine is when I'm thinking about something long enough to really dwell on it, I put my hand across my mouth sideways and start fingering my chin. We've all likely seen a woman twirl her hair when she's driving. That's probably a quirk. Neither are habits, or necessarily bad--they're just quirks.

My wife loves a cup of tea in the morning. That's not her quirk. The quirk is the process of how she prepares it:

- She fills the tea kettle with water and turns the stove on to boil it.
- She runs the hot water faucet until the water is hot and fills her tea cup with it.
- She puts the tea cup with the hot water into the microwave for 2 minutes.
- When the kettle starts to whistle, she dumps the hot water out of the cup, puts a tea bag in it, and then puts the boiling water in the cup.
- She lets the cup sit until it is cool enough to drink.

With most quirks there is neither rhyme nor reason for them, and they can defy logic or reason. Some can be annoying, like the tea cup process is to me. They pose no threat to anyone, they are harmless, and they are just quirks. Discussions about people's quirks are useless. A quirk is here to stay.

When quirks are harmful is when they become sore spots in relationships. Those sore spots can fester and eventually lead to discussions, which can lead to things being said that would have been better not spoken. People are pretty attached to their quirks.

If we allow it to happen, quirks can become wedges in relationships, or worse yet, relationship enders. If we focus on the quirk more than on the person, it can lead to damage in the relationship. When that happens, the person fixated on the quirk may have forgotten about his own quirks which may be annoying to the other party.

Jesus probably came in contact with people who had quirks. Perhaps, even some of the 12 Apostles were quirky. Yet the example He set was simple. Love everyone unconditionally, quirks and all.

Bottom Line Thought: Would you want others to define you by your quirks? Isn't a relationship more important than a harmless quirk or two?

Day 53:
8 Simple Things

8 simple things to make life easier

Make peace with your past. If you don't, there is a good chance it will disturb your present.

What other people think of you is none of your business.

Time heals almost everything. Give it time.

No one is in charge of your happiness—except you.

Don't compare your life with others, or judge them. You have no idea what their journey is all about.

Stop thinking too much. It's alright not to know the answers. They will come to you.

Smile. You don't own all the problems in the world.

Trust God. You are the center of His attention.

Day 54:
Birds Of A Feather

Birds of a feather flock together. That's an old adage, and I'll add that they sure do. I never saw a flock of geese hanging out with grackles. We humans like to do the same thing. We like to hang out or associate with folks that are pretty much like we are. It keeps us in our comfort zone. Don't most of us enjoy meeting and hanging out with people who;

- Are candid, honest, and sincere.
- Have a sense of humor and can laugh at themselves.
- Are humble, show their true selves, and are godly?

We don't like to meet and hang out with those who are obviously;

- liars, scammers, and cheats,
- openly evil or foul and narcissistic people,
- or, chronic self absorbed "down" types.

Something we can consider in every interaction we have with people is to:

Be the kind of people we want to meet.

Some may think that puts us on a road to be exclusionary, that we may purposely be cutting ourselves off from those "lesser" folks. If we live as if we are the kind of people we want to meet, we have those very qualities many others will gravitate to out of a sense of emptiness and longing. And if we are living in that manner, then we will be strong enough to seek out those people who are in need of our example so that our light might shine.

Jesus set the example for us as, throughout His ministry, He always singled out the sinner and downtrodden. Even those He chose to be His 12 Apostles met the qualities of folks we normally wouldn't want to hang out with.

Birds of a feather do flock together. We are all humans, and we all flock together because we are all on a journey. Some are just on a different journey than others, and those who are on the journey of self destruction need all of us others to help them and guide them and pray that they will get on the spiritual journey.

We are all so different, yet we are all so much the same.

Bottom Line Thought: Do you have a heart that will free you to know that you can let your light shine among those who you just don't like or would want as a close friend?

Day 55:
Racism Is Red

In recent times racism has become a hot spot in the news and social media. It's not specific to just these times, because it's been around for a very long time. In broad terms, racism is the poor treatment or violence toward others of a different race, and it is often based on the belief that some races are somehow better than others, or more superior.

I grew up in an area of the country where racism was not only rampant, it was openly obvious. It was the norm and the accepted culture in those states. I was racist and at that time it was all about the color of one's skin. It took many, many years to overcome that racist attitude within me.

Racism isn't about black, brown, yellow, tan, white, or any other color. It's all about red. The hearts of all people of all races are red. There has never been any medical proof that indicates otherwise. Racism is a condition of our hearts. What's in our hearts is what will eventually show in our thoughts, words, and deeds.

Racism is Red!

If we are a closet racist, we are racist, no less so than an openly racist person. If we are racist, how do we change since it is a condition of the heart?

- We look within ourselves, we recognize it, and we claim it.
- Having claimed it, we accept that we have to change that part of us.
- We do that by first acknowledging to ourselves that it is not how God would have us to be, and we forgive ourselves.
- We pray about it, journal about it, share it with trusted Christian friends, and we are transparent about that flaw within us.
- We understand that making this change is a process, just as our spiritual journey is, but we know and trust, that with God's help, we will change.

The change is not easy, and we need to trust that with God's help, everything in our lives is possible.

Bottom Line Thought: Do you see people as people, regardless of the color of their skin? Do you have a red heart for all others who have a red heart?

Day 56:
Sanity On Sunday

I used to dislike going to church. I'd go when I had to, for weddings, Easter and Christmas, baptisms, and funerals. It got in the way of sleeping in on Sunday mornings, going to play golf, or fishing. Those were the excuses I used. The *real* reasons I didn't want to go were;

- I thought that ministers, pastors, and priests were phonies.
    - How could any of them be *that* good as men?
- Those in the congregation were probably just like me, but they were just putting on the Sunday morning show, and were really just phonies.
- Church was for sissies, goodie-goodies, and wimps--something I was not.
- No one there was saying anything I wanted to hear.
    - Preaching was about what was going to happen to me "if"...
- I knew what I was, and there was no way God could love me.
- Church in all aspects just wasn't "real" to me.

I now know that all of those reasons for not going to church and being involved with it were simply wrong, and not true of the church and its people. That came as a result of an amazing spiritual journey.

Those misconceptions are still thoughts in the minds of some men. We have trouble grasping the fact that ministers, pastors, and priests are just the same as we are, men doing a real life's journey, men with baggage, and men who struggle with the same things we do. What has made my, and perhaps yours, church experience so real since my way of thinking was changed, is that the spiritual leaders of those churches, and the folks who go there, are transparent. They too have changed, and are still changing.

Can we perhaps look at church as the clinic, where we can turn ourselves around? It's a place we can go get ourselves a good heaping of Sanity on Sunday, all about real life as it could, and should, be.

Bottom Line Thought: Can you share your church experience with others, so they will be encouraged and want to come try the clinic and get their Sanity on Sunday?

Day 57:
Special Silliness

One nice Saturday afternoon recently, I was waiting outside of the grocery store for my wife to finish shopping. A well dressed older lady came out of the store carrying 2 bags with only a couple of items in each. She waited at the curb next to the pick-up lane for her husband to pick her up. As he started to drive toward her she started to giggle. That was when she stuck her thumb out in a very animated way, as if hitch-hiking. I could see her husband smiling. Then she turned sideways and hiked her dress over one knee and wiggled the knee like a floozy in a movie might do, and started laughing. As he picked her up, they were both laughing loudly, but stopped momentarily to give each other a little kiss before driving off.

As I witnessed that, it was clear that those folks have a happy marriage. They apparently love the silly things, and enjoy sharing silliness with each other and aren't concerned about what others may think about it. That's a special kind of silliness, the kind that can help keep a marriage alive.

During the early years of marriage, we seldom seem to run out of silly little things each partner can do, things meant just for the other, do we? They bring laughter, and a deeply personal bonding between each other takes place. Silly humor helps serve as glue for a happy marriage.

Eventually, things change bit by bit. Everyday life takes its toll. There are pressures of the job(s), finances, and maybe kids. Those things bring a new level of seriousness to the relationship. Each partner must decide if those things need to stand in the way of real happiness, and if they should act like a damper on the partnership. Isn't our real choice whether or not we want to let the marriage become routine, and boring?

It's often been said that humor has a healing effect. From that, can't we believe that a little bit of personal silliness can bring something special to our relationship, something that will help us over those rough edges of the routine and boring?

Bottom Line Thought: Are you struggling with the routine in your marriage? How is your silly factor? If it's not appreciated, does that mean you should stop trying to help keep the marriage alive with some silliness?

Day 58:
The Word Demon

There are times when I'm certain that there's a word demon in my mind. That's the one that tosses some of "those" words into what I'm saying, often at the worst times-- like when the kids are within earshot. That word demon can get us in trouble, right? It's not hard for inappropriate words to come out of our mouths at times like when;

- A discussion with the wife turns into an argument.
- The buddies are over and the stories and joke telling gets out of hand.
- The holiday picnic is going on and discussion turns to the family outcast.
- We're working on something that's broken at the house and something goes wrong.
- We lose our temper with one of the kids in an over the top way.

There are *other* times when the word demon gets us in trouble. Those are the times we *don't* say the appropriate words our kids need to hear from us. The result of not hearing those words will have a more far-reaching impact on their well being and development into adulthood and beyond than the inappropriate ones.

Our kids not only want to hear what is sometimes not spoken, *they need to hear them from us dads*. They need to hear them regularly, with sincerity, honesty, and with enthusiasm. Here are a few examples.

- I am so proud of you.
- I love you so much.
- I am really sorry...
- I forgive you....
- Will you forgive me? I was wrong.
- I am listening to you.
- This is your responsibility.
- You are special in God's eyes.

Bottom Line Thought: Is the word demon having a negative or positive impact in your relationships with your kids? Are you saying the wrong things at the wrong time or the right things at the right time?

Day 59:
Two Options

Pat Riley, currently an NBA executive, was an icon of the sport in his coaching days. He successfully coached the Los Angeles Lakers, the New York Knicks, and the Miami Heat. His success as a coach is easily measured by a resume that few coaches have achieved. A major reason for his success laid in his ability to motivate the players he coached, men making far money than he was. A quote attributed to Riley applies not only to those he coached, but every man, and particularly men who have chosen to improve themselves, to benefit their relationships and spiritual condition.

"There are only two options regarding commitment: you're either in or you're out. There's no such thing as life in between."

If we're going to change and improve ourselves, we need to make a strong commitment to do so. Many things about us will be affected in a positive way, such as:

- Our relationships with our wives and children.
- Our spiritual healing and growth as Christ followers.
- Our own health and sense of well being.
- Our relationships with our parents and all others around us.
- Those who are in need or are hurting.

Commitment is an easy thing to say, but full commitment is difficult, especially with the distractions of today's times and the forces within us that work against it. It is often easy to find an excuse to let our commitment slide just a bit.

God was fully committed to us when He made us. He wasn't in part of the time, or out some of the time. He was all in. His commitment has never wavered. Our commitment to Him will never be perfect because we are imperfect. What is important is that we never fail to keep working on our commitment to Him and trust Him, even though we know we will blow it at times. That is an all in attitude.

Bottom Line Thought: Are you all in, or are you out? Why not search your heart and mind so that you can discover anything that may be preventing you from being all in?

Day 60:
No U-Hauls

An old joke that's been around a long time is that there are no U-Hauls in Heaven. I would add, there's no parking lot for them outside of the Pearly Gates either. The gist of the joke is that you can't take it with you when you die. "It", of course, refers to your stuff, your toys, your fame and accomplishments, or your money.

Most of us know that don't we? And yet, we find ourselves overly focusing on those things at times don't we? It's easy to want more, to be more, and to have more. The "monster of more" plays right into our sense of greed which is really nothing more than a sin. It's recognized as one of the 7 deadly sins in fact. What does any amount of greed within us do to us? It puts us in the position to choose between thinking of ourselves and our stuff and thinking of Godly things that assure us of that place where no U-Hauls are allowed.

Bottom Line Thought: Are you more interested in what you can put into your U-Haul or into your life, your relationships, and walk with God?

Day 61:
The Dog Park

If you're a dog person, have you ever taken your pooch to a dog park? I hadn't until this past year when I took my dog to one. We met Michael, a friend from church, who came with his 2 dogs. There were 4 or 5 other dogs already at the park with their owners when we arrived. Here's what I observed about those dogs all loose in the same area:

- They were all different breeds and ages.
- They varied in size, color, and shape.
- There were differences in physical conditions.

My dog and Michael's dogs had never met before. It appeared that was the case with at least a couple of the other dogs already there, because the owners weren't mingling. This is what was interesting about all of the dogs:

- They got along and played well with each other.
- They acted as if they enjoyed the company of other dogs, and were happy and at peace with their surroundings.
- There weren't any tense moments among the dogs, and none were ignored by the others.
- There was nothing but a whole bunch of happy dog tail wagging going on.

As Michael and I watched the interactions between the 4 legged "strangers", it was clear how different they were from us humans. The comparison showed us what we as humans almost automatically bring to the table with us when we meet and interact with others. We bring our garbage--prejudices, fears, baggage, misconceptions, guardedness, insecurities, biases, and jaded hearts. None of the dogs showed any of that.

We came to the conclusion that our dogs are perhaps less messed up than we are. And we both wondered how much better off this world would be if we just carried less garbage and acted like those dogs.

Bottom Line Thought: Have you thought about what kind of garbage you bring to the table when interacting with others, and what effect it may have on those relationships? Or, are you a happy tail wager?

Day 62:
Jacked Up On Jesus

Doesn't it sometimes seem that the world is out to get you? Things go wrong that shouldn't, people say things they might not mean, etc. Those are days that get to us. Then, once in a while, a day will come when everything is perfect. Those are great days aren't they?

When it's bed time, we go to bed because we know we need the rest for the next day. If it has been one of those "bad" days, it's often hard to get to sleep. We toss and turn and are restless before we finally get to sleep. When that happens to me, I think it's a sign that there is some unfinished business to take care of in my heart before I put the day to rest. I need to take care of that business through prayer.

But what about those days when the day had gone perfectly smoothly, when, at the end, we were full of happiness, love, contentment, and peace? I enjoyed one of those recently. When it came time to go to bed I was exceptionally tired because it was way past my normal time to turn in. I couldn't sleep. I simply couldn't get to that plateau where the body and mind are in sync at the place just before the eyelids close and I drift off to sleep.

I had taken care of my evening prayer so I was sure there wasn't any leftover business to deal with. I got up, sat in my easy chair in the dark house and reflected. The only reason that came to mind for this unusual restlessness was that I was jacked up on Jesus. I felt overwhelmed with His presence in my life, what He had done for me, where my life was heading as a result, and just how far I had come to get where I was now. It was one of the most soul rocking feelings I have had, and it was wonderful.

I think we can all experience those jacked up on Jesus moments if we open ourselves up to fully see and appreciate what His presence means to us. That won't make us one of those so-called "Jesus Freaks." What it will do is make us a much more real Christ follower.

Bottom Line Thought: Have you gotten jacked up on Jesus lately?

Day 63:
Eight Groaks

Men...
Your sons will grow up to be like you.
Your daughters will grow up and marry men like you.
Is that a good thing or a bad thing?

When I was growing up, my Uncle Jimmy said a lot of "Jimmy-ism's. One was *"eight groaks from little grow-corns ache."* It referenced the raising of their four daughters, and it was a take-off on a popular saying, *"great oaks from little acorns grow."* No matter how beautiful a great oak may be, or how ugly and malformed it is, it still came from just one little acorn.

Another old adage about trees goes like this- *"as the twig is bent, so shall the tree grow."* Are we seeing a pattern here that has something to do with raising kids? Let me simplify it. We, the oak tree, produce acorns, from which little trees grow. While those trees are little, they are subject to many things. If they become bent, they will grow up bent.

Our kids can grow up to be great, or they can grow up in many ways less desirable. That is up to us and the choices we make as parents. As dads, working together with our wives, using all of the tools available to us, and keeping spiritual values as our guide, gives us the best shot at raising good kids. Seldom will the child be bent, and thus grow bent.

Our kids emulate us more than we might ever imagine. Their whole early life is one of listening, seeing, absorbing, and finally miming all that we say, are, and do. It's the early impressions that we parents make that has the greatest effect on their later lives as kids, young adults, and finally as adults.

Bottom Line Thought: How would you answer the question at the top given the two statements above it? Are you prepared to make any needed changes before it's too late?

Day 64:
Friends

This is from a meme I saw a while back on Facebook: *"A friend is someone who knows who you are, understands where you have been, accepts who you've become, and gently invites you to grow."* Pretty good stuff isn't it?

Does it sound too "girly" to you? There are men who may think it's too "girly", and by doing so they're missing out on an important presence in their lives, a real friend. We guys have lots of pals and acquaintances. However, because of the barriers we tend to throw up and our lack of transparency, it's hard for us to have a friend as described above. Sometimes, because of circumstances, our wives simply aren't, or can't be, our best friends. This is not to take anything away from the relationship at all. It is simply fact.

There is a saying about friends: *"if we're lucky, we can court our real friends on one hand."* A real friend is one who:

- Will consider your spiritual condition as the most important thing about you.
- You will allow into every corner of your life and mind through your complete transparency.
- Will know your weaknesses and strengths, and will focus on your strengths as he gently guides you through your weaknesses.
- Will appreciate you for what you can be, not what you have done.
- Will diligently work with you as you work to improve your relationships with your wife, your children, and God.

He's a friend who will help you reach a sync point that is missing in your life. That's the place where who you are now, meets the one that, in your heart, you want to be. That type of friend isn't trying to make us like them. God is working through them to make us Godly men. There is no greater kind of love than that.

Bottom Line Thought: Do you have a real friend in your life? If not, why? Are you a real friend to some other? Are you spiritually prepared to be one?

Day 65:
Resentments

Resentment is anger or an over the top displeasure we feel when wronged, insulted, or hurt by others. At times we may even invent reasons for having resentment—like my friend has a happier marriage than I do, or dresses better, etc.

The bad thing about resentments is that they are like scabs—they linger and they can fester, and it's easy to pick them to keep them that way. Those of us, who have had them, know that they can eat away at our insides like some sort of a cancer, especially those we have held for a long time and love to massage. They are troublesome to our relationships because we may think that a particular resentment is in the past--until it pops its ugly head up in the form of sarcasm or spiteful comments. The resentments we carry are often deep within us.

I was talking with a friend the other day and the topic of resentments came up. He offered a couple of comments about them, based on his struggles with them. He said, "Resentments bite only the one holding them", and "having resentments is like taking poison and hoping the other person dies." I agree with what he said.

- If we're carrying resentments, we are ultimately the ones to suffer. They will continue to eat away at us and will feed the flames of any anger we are feeling toward the cause of them. We will continue to be angry and feel bitterness, which robs us of the joy we could otherwise be experiencing.
- We hold the resentments while inwardly wishing, perhaps secretly, ill will on the one responsible for those resentments.

How are we to deal with resentments that we are holding onto? The same way we deal with any other character flaws we have—we prayerfully keep trying to release them through prayer and transparency about them. We recognize them for what they are and what they can do to our spiritual growth, and we don't give up on ourselves while doing whatever it takes to get rid of them.

Bottom Line Thought: Are you carrying any resentment? How do they affect your relationships? What steps can you take to tackle that issue?

Day 66:
Those Pesky Thoughts

Thoughts can zing us can't they? Some thoughts, especially inappropriate ones, pop up at the drop of a hat don't they? For instance, we may look at a nice looking female walking by, and then "those" thoughts come to our minds. Or, someone says something to us and we take it entirely out of context, and we start thinking some angry thoughts, which we know are inappropriate and wrong.

> I'm grateful that some of my thoughts don't appear in bubbles over my head!

There are also times when, right out of the blue, we find ourselves thinking of something so bizarre that it is absolutely unrealistic. We wonder to ourselves, "where in the heck did *that* come from-- that's not me." A lot of the thoughts we have aren't the real us. The evil one knows our hearts and our minds. He also knows our weaknesses and he will use them to our detriment. This is spiritual warfare. The evil one doesn't want us to become more God like. He doesn't want us on our spiritual journeys. He knows we are weak and he wants to keep us that way. Let's recognize a few things about ourselves:

- We will never not have some bad thoughts, and it's impossible to control them. *We just choose not to act on them.*
- We are flawed, and because of that we will have thoughts that surprise us and which are sin centered. *We choose not to act on them.*
- We will never stop either from happening.

So what do we do with those invisible bubble thoughts? We recognize that we will have them, and we accept that spiritual warfare is a real thing within us as we continue our spiritual journey. And, we keep on building our relationship with the God who has made us and who is stronger than any enemy. He is for us. The evil one is against us.

Bottom Line Thought: Are you aware of any spiritual warfare going on in your heart?

Day 67:
Notes

> "I fed the dog before I went to work"
> "Have a great day—you are special"
> "Please remember to pick up the shirts at the cleaners later"
> "I'll pick up Joey after work"

Is there a common thread between the 4 statements? They're all notes that might be written to or by a spouse at any given time. Notes remind us of things we have to do later in the day or are special little personal expressions of endearment for our wife or the kids. There's no sense in feeding the dog twice, so I will leave a note similar to the top one for my wife to see when I leave home early. By the way, he'd eat that second meal in a New York minute.

Notes are like life preservers as well. Some of us have to write notes to ourselves so we remember our wives, mothers, and kids birthdays. It's always better to be a hero because a note reminded us of those important dates, than a goat because we forgot to write a note.

I've found that as I have gotten greyer I'm prone to write more notes than ever—mostly to myself. The past few years I've discovered that my forgeterer works really well, and my rememberer is apparently partially disabled. Notes are a way of life. Nowadays "notes to self" are even easier because of the electronic gadgets of the times we're in. 3-M must be spinning. I wonder if the demand for post-its is down.

Let's set aside my feeble attempts at a little humor to make way for the most serious note you could possibly ever see. It's a note that is, literally, a matter of life and death.

The note tells it all. Maybe we need to see a note like this every day to remind us of His purpose, of where our focus should be, and of how we should be doing life. How soon is soon, we might wonder?

Bottom Line Thought: Are you doing life in such a way that when He does come back, you can stand tall before Him? If you saw that note on your mirror or office wall each day, would it serve as a reminder for you?

Day 68:
Twin Fetus's

In a mother's womb were two babies. One was me, and one was you. One asked the other, "do you believe in life after delivery? Maybe we are here to prepare ourselves for what comes later."

"Nonsense" said the other. "There is no life after delivery. What kind of life would that be?"

The first said, "I don't know, but there will be more light than here. Maybe we will walk with our legs, and eat from our mouths. Maybe we will have other senses that we can't understand now."

The second replied, "That is absurd. Walking is impossible. And eating from our mouths? Ridiculous! The umbilical cord supplies nourishment and everything we need. But the umbilical cord is so short. Life after delivery is to be logically excluded."

The first insisted, "Well, I think there is something and maybe it is different than it is here. Maybe we won't need this physical cord anymore."

The second replied, "Nonsense. And moreover, if there is life, then why has no one ever come back from there? Delivery is the end of life, and in the after-delivery there is nothing but darkness and silence, and oblivion. It takes us nowhere."

"Well I don't know," said the first, "but certainly we will meet Mother and she will take care of us."

The second replied, "Mother? You actually believe in Mother? That's laughable. If Mother exists, then where is She now?"

The first said, "She is all around us. We are surrounded by Her. We are of Her. It is in Her that we live. Without Her this world would not and could not exist."

Said the second, "Well, I don't see Her so it is only logical that She doesn't exist."

To which the first replied, "Sometimes when you're in absolute silence, and you focus, and you really listen, you can perceive Her presence and you can hear Her loving voice, calling down from above.

Source unknown

Bottom Line Thought: What is your take-away from the story as it applies to you?

Day 69:
Just A Second !

"Dad, can you come here? I want to show you something?", he said. I replied, "Just a second." That's when I returned to whatever I was so absorbed with, and forgot about his simple question. I forgot that my son, who I love so much, needed me. There were plenty of those times when the kids wanted me for "just a second" and I blew it. It came full circle recently. I called out for a couple of my adult kids, and they both answered, you guessed it, "just a second, pops." It was then that it hit me as some words from the song *Cat's in the Cradle* popped into my head—"My boy was just like me."

Don't we all "just a second" people in our lives once in a while? We do it with our wives, our kids, and maybe some others. What's the message we send with those 3 words? I believe, at the bottom line, we're saying "whatever I'm doing now is more important than what you need me for." The subtle message it sends is clear-- that we don't view them as important enough, or we don't value them as we should.

There's another area in our lives where we may "just a second" it, perhaps on a regular basis. It's in our relationship with God. If we aren't committed to the sound and firm relationship we need with Him so as to be fully devoted followers of Christ, aren't we in essence saying to Him, "just a second, I'll get to it when I can?" This is all about regularly praying, studying, and growing in Him. Is anything we have to do more important? Is anything more important than Him?

What if this God that made us and the world we live in were to clearly tell us "just a second" as we called upon him in time of need, hurt, or trouble? Or, when we were praying for healing for a family member? If our hearts are right, are we ever more important than others? God may not answer our prayers the way like, or in the timing we want, but He will never say "just a second."

Bottom Line Thought: Do you "just a second" people in your life when it isn't appropriate? How do you think they react? How would you react?

Day 70:
You Can't Close That Door

> When God sees you doing your part, developing what He has given you, then He will do His part and open doors that no man can shut.
> SPIRITUAL INSPIRATION

Most men have busy lives. We work to provide for our family. We try to juggle our free time for such things as taking care of the yard, doing things with our kids and families, having some social time, and getting enough rest. We have a lot going on. Wrapped inside our business of doing life is trying to find time to grow ourselves spiritually.

Time and time again when God has seen us grow spiritually sound, we will find, often with surprise, new doors opening and new challenges which become new beginnings. We may feel stretched as we enter that new territory. The truth is, God doesn't slam doors in our faces. He opens doors for us to shine, to do what He knows we can do for His kingdom. He wants us to use the spiritual gifts He has given us for that purpose. We have to be ready for it and then be ready to roll when He does call. All we have to do is our part—prepare;

- We try to discern what His plan for us is.
- We listen to his leadings.
- We learn what our spiritual gifts are.
- And we use those gifts freely for His work.

It's then that He opens the doors that we can't close, and we can almost hear Him saying, "Enjoy the ride, it's going to be a doozy!"

Bottom Line Thought: Have you found your gifts? If not, what's stopping you? If so, are you using them as He would have you do?

Day 71:
Excuses & Responsibility

We all know someone(s) who we think has an "excuse making gene" in their DNA. You know-- the kind of person who is always pointing a finger at something outside of themselves for any failure, shortcoming, misfortune or mistake that happens. Those are the folks who fail to understand that while they are pointing a finger outward to place blame, there are 3 fingers pointing right back at themselves. Often the excuses they make are quite lame. We do it in our own lives don't we? Sometimes we think that an excuse we offer is the easy way out of a potential jam.

The transition from making excuses on a regular basis to turning into a chronic whiner and complainer is quite easy. There is a subtle difference between the two. That one finger pointing outward will often be pointed at *someone* (at least figuratively) as opposed to some things. In either case, there are still those pesky three fingers pointing straight back at the pointer, as if to say "hey, wait a minute—there is some responsibility *you* have to take in this situation".

As men, it isn't always easy to want to look at our own responsibility when something goes south. For example, there are times when it is easier to want to shift responsibility when there are relational issues, right? In doing so we are feeding our egos and massaging our misguided sense of "superiority." Here's some harsh reality from an unknown source:

> *Everything you do is based on the choices you make. It's not from your parents, your past relationships, your job, the economy, the weather, an argument, or your age that is to blame. You and only you are responsible for every decision and choice you make--Period.*

I wonder if, when we are in the excuse making mode, or turning into whiners and complainers and pointing that finger, how often we are doing it to God as well. And, I wonder if we don't have some pretty lame excuses for not being the Christ followers we could be.

Bottom Line Thought: What kind of an example are you setting for those around you and especially for the kids in your life? Will they know what taking responsibility is when they grow up?

Day 72:
Wrestling With God

Story 1: They were both living in the darkness when they married. They were both good people, it's just that neither was walking with the Lord in their lives. Time passed. He eventually accepted Christ and started the spiritual journey to be a devoted follower of Christ. She remained the same—a nice person, a person others enjoyed being around, a decent person. But, they were unevenly yoked. Each had a world view different from the other. Eventually, as his journey progressed, he fully realized what she was missing in her life. He dreamed of the time when she would accept Christ so they could share a wonderful spiritual journey together. It hasn't happened. They've been married for 37 years. Sometimes the differences in the spiritual side of the marriage caused friction, even though he tried diligently to live his life as an example and give her room to make her choice. He prayed regularly that the Holy Spirit would work in her, to change her. But inside, he was hurting. He was hurting because he knew what she was missing and wanted it so badly for her. He wrestled with God over the situation. He was angry with God because it wasn't happening. He would plead with God to make it happen, and sometimes he just outright asked God why it wasn't happening. He was wrestling with God.

Story 2: His best friend was dying of cancer, and it was a long, slow process. It was sad to see it happening right in front of him. His friend had given so much of himself to help him in his walk with Christ, and there was so much more to do—yet he was now dying. During his last days, he visited his friend. The friend lit up like an over-lit Christmas tree when he came to visit, and none of the conversation that day was about "why me" or "why now." The conversation was all about what a great God we have, one that loves us all so much. It was about all that He has done in our lives, and what was yet to come. It was, given the circumstances, a happy time together. After the visit ended, and he left, he started to wrestle with God. "Why now Lord?" "Why this man Lord?" He was overcome with both sadness and anger, and he hurt.

In both cases, the man was wrestling with God. He felt he was wrong for doing so, until he heard something that made sense of it all. Hurting is something we all experience isn't it? When we are hurt deeply, it can bring us to our knees where we often lash out at God, or plead in deep despair. We are then wrestling with God.

Wrestling with God is a good thing. It's okay to do so. It's spiritually sound to do so, because in doing so we are sharing our rawest pain, our deepest doubts, and our hurt with him. At those times when we are wrestling with Him we are hardly sugar coating anything. We are being our real selves, and that is exactly what He wants from us.

It is during (and after) those times of deep hurt and our subsequent wrestling match with God that we can discover some wonderful things that happen to us as a result.

In story 1 above, he has learned, from sharing with trusted Christian brothers, that God's timing isn't always the same as what we expect or want. Further, he's learned that living the life of a Christ follower is his job, and saving another is God's job, which He will do in His time. Out of that, he's discovered that by wrestling with God he is learning perseverance, which is the stairway to faith, and that the longer he perseveres, the stronger his faith will be.

In story 2, he has learned that sometimes when wrestling with God, there are no good answers that will come of it. But, because he wrestled, he found peace and joy by realizing that it's not a bad thing to wrestle. It's spiritually healthy, because from it comes spiritual strength and a deeper closeness with God.

Bottom Line Thought: Have you thought that it is a bad thing to wrestle with God? If so, in what ways may that have stifled your sense of joy and peace? Has it stymied your faith in God? What might change that?

Day 73:
Getting Up For It

Some mornings we wish we didn't have to get up. The beds are warm, we are comfortable and relaxed, and we are in a huge comfort zone. Yuck--the alarm goes off and we have to get up to start a new day, maybe one we really don't want to face.

Throughout our lives we face situations where we have to "get up for it". They are those pesky times when we know we have to face it here and now and it's something we can't dodge. For example:

- Knowing we're going to have a confrontation with the wife over some bone-head thing we did, one done with good intentions, but it had unintended results.
- Having to have "that" conversation with our young son whom we've noticed is experiencing an affliction which affects all young sons—"raging hormones."
- Having to meet with the boss for a job review when we know we have slacked off more times than we wished, and we know he has noticed it.

We don't have a choice in those situations do we? We have to "get up for it"--just suck it up, then do it, and get it done with. They are involuntary, they must be done.

There are instances in our lives that are more voluntary on our part. Things like whether we're going to go to church or not, whether we will be active in a men's group, how strong of a spiritual leader we will be in our family, and how much time we take to be of help to someone(s) less fortunate than us.

How do we "get up" and stay up for those? They are voluntary things we do, choices, unlike the necessity of facing that discussion with the wife. Anytime anything is by choice and voluntary, there is always an opportunity for laziness and apathy to get in the way.

If we look at <u>all</u> aspects of our spiritual life as a commitment, make that commitment, and continually be aware of that commitment, then it becomes a way of life, and we will find that there isn't any "getting up for it" necessary. It becomes a way of life, a God honoring way of life.

Bottom Line Thought: Do you think that if you are leading a God honoring life that all those other things you may have to "get up" for will be much easier to deal with?

Day 74:
This Too Shall Pass

Every one of us, if asked, could probably say from memory some saying that one or both of our parents used regularly when we were growing up. Some of us would say that we loved hearing it, while others would say they hated hearing it. Either way, I would guess that we would all acknowledge now that they were words of wisdom that our parents shared.

I grew up in a poor family, one that experienced medical issues, hardship, and struggles. I absolutely hated hearing my mother, a woman of strong faith, saying (as she often did), "this too shall pass." For me, a young boy, I never wanted "it", whatever it was that brought out the saying, to happen in the first place. To me, all of the bad in our lives was what was controlling it. And yet, as a youngster in Sunday School I kept hearing how much Jesus loved me. Things didn't compute in the boys mind.

> **THIS TOO, SHALL PASS.**
>
> When things are bad, remember:
> It won't always be this way.
> Take one day at a time.
>
> When things are good, remember:
> It won't always be this way.
> Enjoy every great moment.

Besides the wisdom shared on the graphic, any situation that could cause us to utter "this too shall pass" may help us to discover:

- That we really don't control our own little world.
- Often our expectations far exceed our reality.
- God is in charge of our lives, and we need to listen.
- Our lives will always have some speed bumps and adversity.
- There is *always* joy to be found, we may just have to look for it.

Bottom Line Thought: When faced with adversity, do you let it control you, or do you look at it as a means to grow stronger and build your faith?

Day 75:
Real Men Are Humble

I've wondered how many men think of a humble man as a wimp, a mousy person, a quiet person, a meek man, a sissy, or some combination of those descriptions. I used to think that when thinking of humility, and it boiled down to a baseless description—he just wasn't a man's man. He wasn't "girly", he just wasn't a testosterone laden man. Pretty sad isn't it?

Our view of the characteristics of others is often skewed isn't it? It happens when we have our own ideas, or misconceptions, of what real men are, because we are basing those thoughts on what *we* perceive they should be from our own life experiences and how we view ourselves. It took a long time, and some hard lessons, for me to discover what real humility is. Much of what I thought was not based on any spiritual applications.

I recently heard a message about humility, and it made sense, and it clearly identified those men who I thought of as humble: To be humble, as real men we will:

- Accept the fact that life isn't all about us.
- Decide to serve others and will do, from time to time, random acts of kindness just because we can.
- Learn that humility is an ongoing process, it doesn't just happen.

How do we learn to be humble and live in humility?

- We avoid taking credit. We do things without seeking notice.
- We praise others, and we praise them sincerely and often.
- We help others succeed at what they are doing, and we delight in it.
- We admit our mistakes freely and openly.
- We always try to learn from others.
- We place others before ourselves, we go last.
- We serve others.

We all have available to us an example of perfect humility. The story of Jesus' life here on earth is a picture perfect example of a humble man, and I would guess that no one would ever consider him a wimp! His model of humility exemplifies so well that real men are humble.

Bottom Line Thought: Have you struggled with humility? Has it affected any of your relationships? How might you change and change your view of humility?

Day 76:
The Monkeys in Our Lives

Monkey see, Monkey do. Most of us are familiar with the term. *Wikipedia* says this about the term: "Monkey see, monkey do is a pidgin-style saying that appeared in the American culture in the early 1920's. The saying refers to the learning of a process without an understanding of why it works. Another definition implies the act of mimicry, usually with limited knowledge and/or concern of the consequences."

When we are parents, our kids are playing their own version of monkey see, monkey do every day as they watch us, hear us and innocently incorporate those things into their cache of newly learned stuff. Sometimes those things aren't as charming as a game of patty-cake.

As adults, we sometimes add a 3rd monkey to our routine. It's the monkey hear monkey. That one is a real relationship killer, because he's the one that thrives on gossip, or saying unkind things about others. An example of his two pals, monkey see and monkey do, is when we try, but can't keep up with the mythical Joneses. When we can't keep up with them we might tend to talk about them.

What we need to do as men striving to improve our walk as Christ followers is adopt the good adult monkeys—Monkey don't see, Monkey don't listen, and Monkey don't speak. They will become relationship builders in our tool chest.

Bottom Line Thought: If you're having difficulties once in a while because of monkey see, monkey do, might not it be time to allow them to retire so that you can adopt the 3 adult Don't monkeys? Could your relationships improve by getting that monkey off your back?

Day 77:

Good, Better, Best

On a recent trip to Sears to purchase an appliance, I saw that they are still using signs that say "Good", "Better" and "Best" on the product lines they sell. I suppose it's an okay idea for some. When buying something expensive, I always do my research before going to the store so I will know, for instance, how Consumer Reports rated what I intend to buy. I don't want to rely on what the store says about their products.

The good, better, best thing can apply to our daily lives as men. Let's assume we are trying to be Christ followers and most of our bad decisions and choices are behind us. They've become the baggage in our lives that is in storage simply because it is a part of our story. Besides knee-jerk, now we have available 3 types of decisions and choices we can make—good, better, and best. Sometimes knee-jerk decisions and choices can't be avoided, but if we imbed the trilogy of good, better, and best in our minds and hearts, even those knee-jerk decisions and choices will take on a new and less harmful life.

Let's say we are in a relationship and a conflict has come up. Wouldn't it be helpful to stop and think for a minute: "What's a good way to resolve this?", followed by "If that's a good way, is there a better way that might make us both more comfortable?" Once we've answered that, what if we asked ourselves; "Is this the best way to resolve this so that we *will* be comfortable with the results, with no damage to the relationship?" It may sound convoluted, but can't our first choices and decisions, which can be good ones on their face, fall short of what might be an ideal solution?

Sometimes we just don't know what the outcomes will be of those choices and decisions. Sometimes the best may seem to be a real stretch for us. That is where faith comes in. Good, better, and best applies to faith as well:

Little faith (good) says: "God can do it."

Big faith (better) says: "God will do it."

Great faith (best) says: "It is done, for nothing is impossible with God."

Bottom Line Thought: If you feel you are in routine mode when making decisions and choices, are you open to trying the good, better, best approach?

Day 78:
Folsom Prison Blues

Johnny Cash is an icon in the country-western music world. His signature song, *"Folsom Prison Blues,"* was released in 1955 and it rose to the top of the charts like a rocket ship. Cash knew all about hard times, both in life and in prison.

Prisons aren't nice places. It was especially true when Cash wrote that song. We wouldn't want to be there would we? I can't imagine what goes on inside those places, where everything is a system within the system, where folks have to be on guard and fear for their wellbeing. According to a friend of mine whose dad was in one of those "cushy" prisons for white collar crime, even they are not nice.

Consider this—we all live in a prison(s) of sorts. Yes, you read it right.

- At times we are prisoners to time or the clock more than we want to be.
- We can be held prisoner by the "monster" of more, or his close relative, "I want it now!"
- Some of us are prisoners to a rancid relationship.
- We can be held prisoner by our own baggage and stuff.
- Our habits and our sin hold us prisoner.

Some of us are held in maximum security at the worst prison there is. This is the prison that keeps us locked up, where we experience no real freedom at all. Its name is "fear of what others think." When we're in this prison, our spiritual growth is stifled. While a prisoner there, we:

- Can't be all that God wants us to be.
- Find it's hard to do what is right instead of what is popular.
- Can't live to our fullest potential.
- Find it's hard to be transparent with others.
- Experience issues that don't need to happen in our relationships.
- Have a hard time developing a deep and lasting relationship with Christ.
- Can't be real, as we truly were made to be.

Once we escape from the maximum insecurity of this prison, our visits to all of those others will diminish, and we will be totally free, never again to sing the *"Folsom Prison Blues."*

Bottom Line Thought: Are you being held captive by anything? Does it interfere with your being real, transparent, and true? What can you do to free yourself?

Day 79:
Truth In Advertising

Years ago a law called the "Lemon Law" was passed to protect the consumer when buying a used car. At the time, used car salesmen were quite unscrupulous and it wasn't uncommon for them to sell a "pig dressed up in a prom dress" to an unsuspecting buyer. Nowadays, almost all products are labeled to the max, including descriptions, ingredients, and warnings when called for.

With all the labeling, it's called truth in advertising and its intent is to protect consumers. Even with truth in advertising, there continues to be scammers who will continue to find ways to cheat his fellow man. The brokenness of man, in evidence since Adam and Eve, still thrives in today's times. The Bible is full of stories of the brokenness of mankind. If lemon laws were applied to mankind, we'd all be in trouble wouldn't we?

As we have read and/or studied our Bibles, have any of us ever read any disclaimers or warnings anywhere in it? Of course we haven't. God's word needs no truth in advertising. It is what it is—God's word. Have any of us ever felt cheated or disappointed from reading our Bible? Again, it's God's word, and it has withstood the test of time. It's one tool for our tool chest of life that won't be covered by any lemon law or fail to meet truth in advertising.

Bottom Line Thought: Isn't it amazing how much God loves you, flaws and all? Are you grateful that the Bible is the ultimate in truth in advertising-- that God's word is the real deal?

Day 80:
Grackles

A few times a day we feed the "critters" that hang around our yard. It's fun to be inside on a nasty wintery day and watch the squirrels and the birds co-existing pleasantly as they feed on the stuff we put out in the side yard. The squirrels in particular are fun to watch because they seem to have a great playtime when it is feeding time.

In the blink of an eye, the whole scene changes as the neighborhood bullies and thugs swarm in and take over. The grackles have arrived. They're a bit larger than blue jays, and meaner. They don't come in small groups. There may be as many as 25 to 30 in the pack, and when they come around the squirrels and pretty birds scatter, leaving the food for the grackles to chow down on.

Fortunately, grackles are easily frightened. All we have to do is stand by the window and wave a hand and they all fly off immediately off to a nearby tree. This is what they do:

- They lurk in the background, always nearby.
- They come in and disrupt.
- They try to steal the good stuff.
- They are very patient—they will make foray after foray.

That swarm of black ugly grackles is like the sin and evil in our lives isn't it, always lurking nearby, ready to pounce at any time. It disrupts our spiritual lives, or tries to. It tries to steal our hearts and harden it, and is very patient. It never seems to rest. But, unlike the grackles, we can't just wave it off can we?

Bottom Line Thought: Can you recognize the grackles in your life? How do you deal with them?

Day 81:
Money

We all enjoy money to one degree or another. Some enjoy it more than others. It controls some, and others control it. It's a necessary thing in our daily lives. Money's been around for a long time, even way back in biblical times. There are many references to money in the Bible, all of which are to teach us to treat it wisely and not let it interfere with our relationship to God.

Here's a little story about money from an unknown source, which was used to paint a life picture:

A well known speaker started off one of his seminars holding up a $20.00 dollar bill. In the room of 200 attending the seminar, he asked, "Who would like this $20.00 bill?" Hands started going up—lots of hands. "I'm going to give this $20.00 to one of you, but first let me do this." He proceeded to crumple up the bill. He then asked, "Who still wants it?" And again, the hands started rising. "Well", he said, "what if I do this?" and he dropped the crumpled bill on the floor and started to grind it into the floor with his shoe. He picked it up, now very crumpled and dirty, and asked once again, "Now who still wants it?", and once again the hands went up into the air.

He paused for one of those pregnant moments and looked over the audience. "My friends," he said, "there was a valuable lesson to learn there. No matter what I did with the money, you still wanted it because it did not decrease in value. It was still worth $20.00. Many times in our lives we are dropped, crumpled, and ground into the dirt by the decisions we make and the circumstances that come our way. We may never feel as though we are worthless, because no matter what has happened, or what will happen, you will never lose your value."

Dirty, clean, crumpled or crushed, we are all priceless to God. The worth of our lives doesn't come from what we have done, but in who we are—a child of God. Some are not in relationship with Him, but that will never diminish the love He has for us. Maybe we just need to hear the message of ouir worth to Him to break free of whatever it is that is holding us back.

Bottom Line Thought: Can you be like the money man, the messenger of who we really are?

Day 82:
A Flat Tire

Getting a flat tire is a pain in the neck isn't it? They never occur at a good time. When they happen, we are faced with a choice—call someone to put the spare on or do it our self. Either way, someone's going to get dirty. The whole episode of getting a flat just isn't nice.

If we don't pay attention to our tires, can't we expect that eventually they may either wear out or that we could get an unexpected flat? Worse yet, if we abuse the tires by hitting debris in the road or drive across pot holes, doesn't it seem reasonable that we might get a flat tire? Of course it does. So what do we do to minimize the possibility of getting a flat tire? We keep aware of their condition and we avoid abusive driving on them.

In some ways a marriage is like the tires on our cars. If we don't pay attention to it, it can go flat. When we are newly married, our marriage is like the new set of tires on the car—perfect, and fit for the long run. As the marriage grows older, our attention is on other things as well—jobs, the family, financial issues, etc., and we can easily start to miss or ignore some of the wear patterns. If we neglect those, the marriage will go flat. Many pastors and marriage counselors are well aware of the words, "our marriage is flat."

If we don't pay regular attention to the tires on our car, or are careless in how we protect them, we can expect that eventually we will experience a flat tire. It's no different in a marriage or relationship.

Bottom Line Thought: Have you experienced the aggravation of having a flat tire? Did you enjoy it? How do you think you would react, and what would you do if your marriage went flat? Are there some things you can change to help keep it vibrant and alive so it doesn't go flat?

Day 83:
Potato Or Egg?

Circumstances are unavoidable. Loosely speaking, a circumstance is a fact or condition that affects a situation. If we find ourselves in a situation, good or bad, there are circumstances that factor into the situation. How we react to or resolve the situation is all on us and the choices and decisions we make. The circumstances are present, and they are not in our control. What is in our control is how we resolve the situation.

If that sounds gibberish, then perhaps this analogy will help shed some light on it:

> *"The same boiling water that softens the potato hardens the egg. It's not about the circumstances, but rather what you are made of."*
>
> Source unknown

The world (boiling water-circumstance) can either harden our hearts (egg) or soften our hearts (potato). It's not about the world. It's about us, in spite of the world, making the choice to have a softened heart (a heart for God) or a hardened heart (a worldly heart). It's our choice.

Bottom Line Thought: Like it or not, you are in the world, and you can't change that. In what ways might you be letting worldly things condition your heart?

Day 84:
Dear Porn Daddy

Supposedly, the following unedited letter was a real letter, sent by a married woman to her father. It had been posted on a parenting blog and made anonymous due to the subject matter. It took a lot of guts to write it, and even more to send it to her dad. I can't imagine how he felt when he read it.

As I read it, several thoughts came to mind:

- *Our children are far more perceptive than we think they are.*
- *They see and hear a lot more than we realize.*

"Dear Dad:

I want to let you know first of all that I love you and I forgive you for what this has done to my life. I also wanted to let you know exactly what your porn use has done to my life. You may think that this affects only you, or even your and mom's relationship. But it has had a profound impact on me and all of my siblings as well.

I found your porn on the computer somewhere around the age of 12 or so, just when I was becoming a young woman. First of all, it seemed very hypocritical to me that you were trying to teach me the value of what to let into my mind in terms of movies and music, yet here you were entertaining your mind with this junk on a regular basis. Your talks to me about being careful with what I watched meant virtually nothing.

Because of pornography, I was aware that mom was not the only woman you were looking at. I became acutely aware of your wandering eye when we were out and about. This taught me that all men have a wandering eye and can't be trusted. I learned to distrust and even dislike men for the way they perceived women in this way.

As far as modesty goes, you tried to talk with me about how my dress affects those around me and how I should value myself for what I am on the inside. Your actions, however, told me that I would only ever truly be beautiful and accepted if I looked like the women on magazine covers or in porn. Your talks with me meant nothing and, in fact, just made me angry.

As I grew older, I only had this message reinforced by the culture we live in. that beauty is something that can only be achieved if you look like 'them.' I also learned to trust you less and less as what you told me didn't line up with what you did. I wondered more and more if I would ever find a man who would accept me and love me for me and not just a pretty face.

When I had friends over, I wondered how you perceived them. Did you see them as my friends, or did you see them as a pretty face in one of your fantasies? No girl should ever have to wonder that about the man who is supposed to be protecting her and the other women in his life.

I did meet a man. One of the first things I asked him about was his struggle with pornography. I'm thankful to God that it is something that hasn't had a grip on his life. We still have had struggles because of the deep-rooted distrust in my heart for men. Yes, your porn watching has affected my relationship with my husband years later.

If I could tell you one thing, it would be this: porn didn't just affect your life. It affected everyone around you in ways I don't think you can ever realize. It still affects me to this day as I realize the hold that it has in our society. I dread the day when I have to talk to my sweet little boy about pornography and its far reaching greedy hands, how pornography, like most sins, affect far more than just us.

Like I said, I have forgiven you. I am so thankful for the work that God has done in my life in this area. It is an area that I still struggle with from time to time, but I am thankful for God's grace and also my husbands. I do pray that you are past this and that the many men who struggle with this will have their eyes opened.

Love, your daughter"

Bottom Line Thought: Of everything that we men do, any interest we may have in pornography is probably the most closely held secret we carry. We are sure that it is only known to us. Maybe that's not really the case, as indicated by the letter above. If you are struggling with it, or are tempted by it, have you considered measures that you could take to help overcome it? Have you thought of the possible consequences of it on your relationships? Have you considered that it is a road block to being a truly godly man?

Day 85:
A Door Stop

A young man rang the door bell at the house one evening. When I opened the door, I found he was trying to sell us a cable TV package. I explained that we were quite happy with the set up we had and weren't interested. It seemed as if the man didn't want to hear that. As he got increasingly persistent in his sales pitch, I found that politeness didn't appear to faze him, so I ended up getting a bit rude to get him to finally leave. I didn't slam the door shut on him, but I came close.

At communion the following week I was reminded of another door that I control. It's the door to my mind and heart. It's the door to God that I shut too often. As the bread was passed, we were encouraged to open the door to Him and deeply thank Him for all the ways we saw Him at work in us during the past week. I realized then just how much I had shut the door on Him all my life. And I realized something else which came to me quite strongly. At those special times (communion), I had always had a huge sense of gratitude because Christ died for *us*. On this day however, I made it personal—Christ died for *me*, and a whole new level of emotion captured me. As the cup was then passed, we were asked to focus on that door during the upcoming week in order to specifically see God at work in our lives during that time.

A prayer came to mind right then "Lord, let me keep a mental door stop handy, so that I don't shut You out selectively during my time here on earth, so that I can't close the door. I need to constantly see Your work in my life each day."

A door stop in the mind and heart isn't to keep the pest out. It's to let the Best in.

Bottom Line Thought: Sometimes we lose track of the door stop don't we? The one that lets the Best in, that is. What might you be missing out on if your door to God is shut more often than you would like?

Day 86:
I've Got Your Back

At the church I attend, I've found that the services are never boring. In fact, quite the opposite—they are relevant, exciting, and the messages are always thought provoking. The topic of a pre-Christmas message was "A family tree full of knots." Briefly, it addressed the family tree of Jesus as documented in the book of Matthew as a build up toward the Christmas story. Jesus' family tree was pretty messed up—there were a lot of knots in that tree. We were taken back through the lineage and the associated back stories, and were shown not just a lot of goodness, but some pretty awfulness that was in evidence as well.

I've never had an appreciation for genealogy, and therefore don't know a lot about my own lineage. I do know this with certainty—our recent clan has its share of knots in the family tree, including me. We don't have to go back very far to discover that. Actually, none of us do, do we? Brokenness isn't an individual or family thing is it? It's a thing that has affected all of mankind, since the days of Adam and Eve.

It might make us wonder why Matthew included all of that stuff as a precursor to the Christmas story he wrote. It was included to show that <u>*God is bigger than our mistakes*</u>—all of them. There's a direct lesson there for our everyday lives:

- Our current lives are more than our pasts.
- Our lives are about what we choose to do next.
- Because God says, "I've got your back!"
    - o "you are redeemed"
    - o "I know all about the past"
    - o "I still want you for my purposes."

It's really that simple, yet don't some of us still have a hard time dealing with our past? Don't we find it difficult to keep ourselves forward focused instead of looking backwards? All we really need to do is praise Him and trust Him because He has our backs.

Bottom Line Thought: Knots add definition and beauty to wood when it's cut for use, particularly in furniture. Can you look at your knots as beautiful, and know that they are so because God truly has your back?

Day 87:
Never Gonna Win!!

Some of us are NASCAR fans. I'm an unabashed rabid fan of the sport, perhaps in part because of my southern roots. One year I was able to receive NBC television credentials before going to the track, and because it was considered a "hot" pass I was afforded unlimited access to areas not normally visited by the fans. A benefit of that pass was that I was able to view the race from the pit stall of one of the top names. But one of the most exciting benefits was the freedom to roam around prior to the race and meet and talk with some of the drivers, one of which was Michael Waltrip, a racer with a unique story.

Michael won the Daytona 500 in 2001. That win was his <u>first</u> win out of 443 starts over a span of 12 years. He raced a full schedule (36 races per year) for all of those years always confident that he would win. He never gave up trying.

Aren't there times in all of our lives when we think we're just not going to win? We feel, at times, like shouting out loud "I'm never gonna win?" This race to the finish, that time when we know we can be with God for eternity, gets all botched up, and we feel like failures. Fear of the unknown stops some good decisions we might make. Sometimes we are our own worst enemies in that race of life. Sometimes the easy way out might seem the only way out—to just quit. That's the course the evil one wants us to take.

Waltrip was never gonna win—if he gave up. His goal for every single one of those 443 races was to win. He wasn't out there to drive a pretty car around a track at high speeds. He was there to win.

We are not here in our world to just occupy space and time anymore than Waltrip was. No matter what our spiritual condition is at any given time, nor how much spiritual warfare is within us, this is our race to win—<u>no matter what</u>. But, we're never gonna win it if we give up.

Bottom Line Thought: Have you defined your race of life? Are you prepared to win at all costs?

Day 88:
Well?

This is short and sweet, but a lot to think about:

If we meet someone for the first time, how long will it take them to figure out that we're a Christian?

Does the answer to that question change any if the meeting didn't take place in church or with a church group?

Here's another thought provoking question;

If we were arrested for being a Christian, would there be enough evidence to convict us?

Bottom Line Thought: Do you wear your faith on your sleeve or do you have an off and on switch somewhere convenient? Are you a chameleon with your Christianity, does it change according to who you are with or where you are at?

Day 89:
Walls

I've had the opportunity to work in the construction business. When building a house, the walls are easy to construct. They're laid out on the sub-floor, the bottom and top plates marked for the studs, and then the studs are nailed in place. A whole exterior wall is made on a flat surface like that, and when completed it's simply raised up, put in place, braced, and nailed to the decking. On to the next wall, and before you know it the four exterior walls are completed and are attached. The interior walls, for the rooms, come next and follow the same process. The walls are, in a sense, barriers or borders.

When we get down to it, whether we are builders or not, we've all built walls haven't we? The walls we've built aren't built with wood or bricks however. They're built with will and determination, and sometimes guilt and shame. They're the walls we build within us, around our hearts. While others can't physically see the walls we've built, they often know they are there. Here are some thoughts on the walls we build:

- We build strong walls around that place within us where we keep hidden all of our darkest secrets about ourselves—the ones we want no one else to know about.
- We build walls around our emotions because we don't want to appear "soft" or "unmanly."
- We build walls around our past, much like junkyards that have fences around them, to hide the debris.
- We build walls around the "real" us, the part of us we don't want our church friends to see or know about.

While our walls are fairly easy to build, there is one wall that is particularly easy to build. It's the wall around all of our other walls; the one that we hope protects those other walls from being seen. It's called our phony selves, the show we put on for all others to show them how "normal" we are. God knows all about our walls because He sees right through them. And He knows that the more transparent we are with Him, the less we will need any of those other walls. And if He is our foundation, there is no need for any walls.

Bottom Line Thought: How can you go about tearing down some of your walls?

Day 90:
Life-ism's

I love collecting little life gems—short sentences about life that pack a punch, like the following;

"It doesn't matter what you can't do with what you don't have."

"I follow Jesus. When I'm dead, you'll know I caught up to Him."

"When you let go of what you are, you become what you might be."

"Mistakes have the power to turn you into something better than you were before."

Maybe you're like me. Whenever I find one of those gems, I try to retain it as a life-ism. They are short and sweet, get right to the point in their simplicity, and can zing that part inside of me that needs zinging. Often times we will see ourselves in them—if not what we are now, then perhaps how we would like to be.

One other thing about life-ism's; they aren't preachy or judgmental. They are just facts laid out there for us to see and think about. They address the man within us, the one we yearn to be.

Bottom Line Thought: Have any life-ism's struck a chord with you lately? Are you on the lookout for them in your daily routine?

Day 91:
Seasons

Each of Ma Nature's seasons is different, and each affects us differently. When she's tossing us a cold spell with below freezing weather that goes on for a while, we tend to long for those comfortable spring days when we can be out in our yards. And, when we are sweltering in the worst days of the dog days of summer, we can't wait for fall to come with its brilliant colors and cooler temperatures. We also tend to think about and prepare for each of the seasons in advance of when they come about.

Life has its seasons as well, but perhaps we don't place as much importance or thought into those seasons as we do with Ma Natures. The seasons of life are:

- Spring—birth to the 20's
- Summer—20's to 40's
- Fall—40-'s to mid 60's
- Winter—mid 60's till our death.

Each of those life seasons play a role in our lives, and there is a lot of flexibility in the spring through fall seasons. All of those are important to us. It is what we do in those seasons that prepare us for our final season of life, the winter. There are many things we can do right, and there .are an equal amount of things we can do wrong during those seasons, and each one can be a tipping point of how our end days will be. Some of the more important preparations that should be addressed in those first three seasons of our lives are:

- How are we relationally with our families and those close to us?
- Have we prepared ourselves financially?
- Is our spiritual foundation solid; are we in community with God?
- Have we prepared ourselves intellectually and emotionally for the winter season?

I know from experience, and perhaps you do as well, that the invincibility of youth doesn't last forever. Sometimes we don't think about that winter season soon enough, and when it comes we're going to say one of two things; "oh gosh," or "oh thank goodness." One thing is certain—the clock will run out, and old age will be upon us, and if we aren't prepared, life will be much more difficult.

Bottom Line Thought: Are you thinking and preparing for the winter season of your life?

Day 92:
Broken Crayons

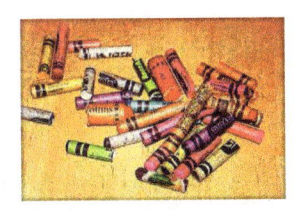

Do you remember your first box of crayons? Did you have the "real" crayons, the Crayola brand, or did you have those "other" ones that weren't as nice? I remember thinking someone was king of the hill when they got the big box, the one with 48 crayons inside. We were poor, so I had to settle for the little box.

What happened when a crayon broke? What would we do with it? Of course, we'd save it or maybe try to tape it together. They were still useful, and we could color with the pieces. The fact that they were broken didn't really matter too much to us did it?

Our lives are like those crayons. God has plenty of uses for the broken pieces that are us—if we just let Him use us. I have seen men who have been broken in a major way paint beautiful pictures of a Godly life once they accepted their past and walked with a forward focus.

God knows where each of us is broken like those crayons, and He knows that our broken pieces can still color. All He asks is that we continue to color our own little corner of the world with our own examples of His grace and love so that others can see those wonderful works of art.

Bottom Line Thought: What's stopping you from picking up your broken pieces and drawing a work of art from God for others to see?

Day 93:
Goose Church

Nothing against Canadians, but they can keep the geese named after them. Canadian geese are beautiful, but they have become way too domesticated over the years and have all but taken over any open green areas—like golf courses. Their debris is, well, yucky.

There's one thing about geese that intrigues me. I like to watch them flying. When the flocks (to be correct, gaggle) are flying, they fly in a majestic vee formation. The flight is never interrupted as the goose at the head of the vee suddenly drops out of the lead and the next goose in line takes its place at the head. Meanwhile, the leader that dropped out falls back to the tail end of the vee and resumes formation flying from there. Those vee formations are a great example of the old saying, *"the whole is the sum of its parts."*

Our church is like those geese. No, not the messy part, but like the flying formation part. It's a place where the whole is the sum of its parts in the truest sense of the word. It's all about "our church", not this church, or this place. There is no head goose. No one goose is any better than any of the other geese, and everyone pitches in to make it work. It has a bare minimum of staff, yet the flock is large. Each of the pastors is just another goose in the flock. And, all of us geese are in full agreement—we are each broken in our specific ways and in need of fixing, and that is why we flock together. Since each goose shares in various roles, the flock continues to fly uninterrupted and toward its destination.

Many of us have been to churches where we felt less than equal, or perhaps inferior, or the guilt card was played. I found it was hard to be happy and feel sincerely welcomed in those places.

By the way, the reason geese fly in formation and switch off leading is that they instinctively know they are all equal, and they share equally in the burden of reaching the end of their journey. That's exactly what the geese in my gaggle (church) do.

Bottom Line Thought: Are you happy in your church experience? Or, do you sometimes feel like an outsider looking in?

Day 94:
What's New?

During our lifetimes we buy quite a bit of new stuff don't we? Sometimes the stuff we buy isn't actually new-new, but it is new to us. Some of the new things we buy are homes, cars, cell phones, computers and electronics, clothes, and more.

What do we do when we buy new stuff? We take care of it and maintain it. We fix things around the house, we take care of our cars so they last, and we are careful with our clothes. We don't beat up our cell phones, and electronics, so that we can continue to use and enjoy them. We do it because our stuff is important to us.

We are told as Christians, when we accept Christ and believe that He died on the cross for our sins, *we are made a _new_ person, and we are born again.*

All of our stuff, the things we buy new, will eventually age and become unusable, in spite of the care we give it. It may take years, but eventually there is little maintenance that can be done to prolong its useful life any further. Sometimes, because of its age, we will give it away or trade whatever it is in for a new one.

When we are made a new person, do we treat our new self like our stuff, letting it eventually get old, worn out, and of diminished value? Of course we don't. We are so thankful that we aren't what we once were that we strive to maintain our new selves until our dying day.

Isn't it great to know that when God made us new;

- He didn't make junk.
- The new we will wear out only if we choose to let it.
- The maintenance program for our new selves is really quite simple.

What kind of rewards do we get when we buy new stuff? It's nothing like the reward we get (heaven) by becoming the new person we became when we were born again is it? One more thing—we all get a lifetime warranty on the new person we became, in this life and beyond, as long as we maintain it.

Bottom Line Thought: Do you take care of the new you better than you take care of your stuff?

Day 95:
The Perfect Marriage

The above paragraph describes the perfect marriage clearly and concisely. Whoever wrote it knew exactly how to phrase it wouldn't you say? Talk about insight!

In our heart of hearts I think we all know there is no such thing as a perfect marriage. There are certainly some very good marriages, some great ones in fact, and some bad marriages. Each partner in a marriage enters into it with some baggage, and it's not unusual for the marriage itself to be the cause for some more given the dynamics of two people living together. There are a gazillion books on the market about marriage, and an equal amount of psychobabble on how to achieve success in your marriage or how to make the most of your marriage. The bottom line at best is, marriage;

- Is not easy
- Takes a lot of work by both parties
- Needs a strong commitment by each partner
- Will not always be fun and enjoyable
- Is not the fairytale life we often envision when young
- Gets tired and boring at times
- Requires times of compromise
- Needs openness and transparency
- And, to be solid, it needs God as its foundation.

There is one marriage manual we can all lean on to help guide us as we work toward making our marriages perfect. It's called the Bible.

We don't need to bemoan the fact that our marriages aren't perfect. There should be great joy in knowing that two imperfect and committed people are taking a lifelong journey together, with Christ in the center, *no matter what comes to stand in the way.*

Bottom Line Thought: If you accept the fact that you are not perfect, but rather a work in progress, how hard can it be to think of your marriage in the same way?

Day 96:
Dumping

An unfortunate incident took place between a cab and a truck. The cab had stopped at a stoplight. Shortly thereafter a truck stopped for the light next to the cab. The truck was loaded with manure, and when it stopped some of the load shifted and much of it, in fact a lot, ended up spilling over onto the cab. Needless to say, it was a big mess.

Our lives are like that cab at times. We get dumped on, just as we sometimes may dump on someone else. I'm not referring to what might be called "good dumping." I'm talking about the kind of dumping that is based on rumor, innuendo, false or misinformation, or a dump that arises out of anger. This kind of dumping can be actively open dumping or it can be stealth dumping where we cover our tracks so as not to be found out as the source. Nothing good comes out of it, and it can create a big mess in the life of the one dumped on. It's particularly bad because it is almost always done intentionally. We're not talking here about dumping our problems on others—we're talking about smack talk, or trash talk.

God realized that we humans were going to be dumpers and dumpees, that we were going to reveal the ugliness available to humans from time to time. Why else would the following have been included in the prayer of prayers, the Lord's Prayer?

>..."and forgive us our trespasses as we forgive those who trespass against us"...

Dumping on others is just another form of sin. We are not lifting the dumpees up. Rather, we are tearing them down, just as we are being sinned against when we are being torn down by others. What is crucial is how we react and what we do when it occurs.

Maybe it would help us all if we changed things just a little bit, to something like;

> "Lord, forgive me for trash talking John. Remind me that Jerry sought forgiveness when he bad mouthed me."

Bottom Line Thought: Do you catch yourself dumping on someone at times? How do you react when you find you have been the recipient? Do you end the dumping with forgiveness, or do you harbor it and let it affect the relationship?

Day 97:
One Sided Conversation

He said, "You know, I call myself a Christian. I accepted Christ as my Lord and Savior. I was happy and content, but then, I walked away from it all. I stayed away for a number of years, and finally came back. I have a much clearer idea now of what grace and redemption is, and where I stand. My relationship with God is much stronger now because I realize that He never left me when I left Him. I'm at ease now, more than I have ever been. I know that I still sin, and it bothers me—a lot. I share those sins in prayer with God, and pray that he will give me the strength to overcome them. I have some Christian brothers with whom I share my brokenness and we talk about God's grace. Sometimes that is not enough. The truth is, I am plagued by my propensity to continue sinning and do things which aren't Christ like. Like Paul, I can't stop doing those things which I shouldn't do, and I often can't do the things that I need to do, and it confuses me because I consider myself a Christian. At those times I feel hypocritical. I love my "new" life in Christ, and I enjoy my journey, but I hate the fact that I am so weak. I know that I am in a better way, that my heart is softer, that my head is clearer, and that as a result I am a better man than I ever was. Yet, deep inside I feel that I am somehow a failure because I still do things and behave in ways that don't glorify the very God that saved me in the first place."

How often have we had a similar conversation with ourselves? You see, this was a conversation I had with myself one day as I was walking the dog. At first glance we might think it was coming from one real messed up guy. In reality though, it's a very bold and brutally honest conversation. It is a sign of acknowledgement that the more we know about ourselves, the more we need to know. And, it is a sign of good solid Christian growth of someone on the trail from being a spiritual baby to one who is spiritually mature.

Bottom Line Thought: Could you have a one sided conversation with yourself to help you clear up some inner confusion about yourself?

Day 98:
A Fool and His Money

"A fool and his money are soon parted." I grew up hearing that often, I suppose because we were poor. The rebellious me didn't like hearing that, so much so that if I managed to get a dollar it would be spent in a New York minute (no offense to New York). As a result I, perhaps like many of us, have always had difficulty managing money.

At times church has a way of bringing truths to life for us doesn't it? In a great "ah-ha" moment a while back I heard 2 of those truths that apply to possessions and money;

1. "The way we view God determines how we do life."
2. "All you think you own, you owe."

The fools first thought is on himself. Later, if there is time and inclination, there will be some thought about God. And he only gives grudging acknowledgement, if any, that God has blessed him with his stuff and his money. He's happier with the knowledge that he did it on his own.

It can be easy for us to fall into that trap can't it? Sometimes it's not easy or pleasant to think, let alone act, on sound biblical principles of money management, including sharing it for Kingdom purposes. If God is truly at the core of our lives, we will do our life according to those principles, and our thinking will change to knowing we owe for all we have, that our money and our stuff isn't ours—it is just on temporary loan to us.

After many years, I am a fool whose money is soon parted from, just as I would hope many of us are-- because it is departed the right way. There's a deep sense of joy in knowing that the dearly departed money is being used for kingdom purposes instead of just accumulating stuff for me.

Bottom Line Thought: As one of the bank ads ask, "where is your wallet?" Are you inclined to open that wallet to share with your church, with people in need, and with causes that will further Kingdom work?

Day 99:
Drop It

What would the world be like today if?

- God hadn't sent His son, Jesus, to save the world, and
- If Jesus had stuck to carpentry instead of ministry, and
- If, during His ministry He hadn't come across some fishermen at the sea of Galilee, and
- Told those fishermen to "leave everything and follow me", and
- They had refused?

Many of us will recognize that scenario as the story of the beginning of the relationship between Jesus and the disciples, whose task it was to spread the word through their ministries to grow Christianity. They didn't balk, they didn't ditch Him, they dropped their fish, they followed Him, and from that point on Christianity grew.

It's now 2015. How do we react as Jesus tells us, yet today through His word, to drop everything and follow Him? What will the world be like in 2075, 2250, or even 3400 if we, unlike those disciples, refuse?

It's great to call ourselves Christians. It's better to *be* a Christian and live like one. Those who aren't Christians can't go to a store and buy it. Christianity isn't a "getting" thing; it's a giving thing—from person to person as in the days of the disciples. If we don't share our Christianity with others, how will it ever continue to grow? When we are told to drop everything, some of those things are;

- the importance we put on our stuff
- our comfort zone
- our fear of being different
- our doubts about ourselves

When we are told to follow Him after dropping everything, we are being told to follow the example He showed here on earth by doing that one on one thing of spreading His word to make more Christians.

Bottom Line Thought: More so than ever, we need to, in any big or little ways, share our faith with others. Can you be a disciple in today's times?

Day 100:
To-Do Lists

When we are busy people, or, like me, getting older, we make to-do lists. They become important so that we don't forget things, (and if we are careful we will remember where we placed the list so we can use them.)

Sometimes those lists become a bit overwhelming for us, don't they? We will get an empty sheet of paper out and with real enthusiasm jot down lots of stuff we have to get done—and it doesn't always work out does it? At times it is like eating at a good buffet--we bite off more than we can chew.

Overall, lists are good and serve their purpose. The give us a plan to follow for the day's activities, a sequence of mostly important stuff we should get done. They help keep us focused on the important stuff as we run through the course of our daily lives.

There's another to-do list that can help us greatly. Since we are striving to be better men, often facing any number of challenges to our spiritual condition as we go about our daily lives, a simple to-do list could help us cross the hurdles we run into;

Today's To-Do List
#1 Practice kindness.
#2 Let go of what I can't control.
#3 Count my blessings.
#4 Listen to the Holy Spirit.
#5 Walk with God.
#6 Live like Jesus.
#7 Pass this on to encourage someone else.
iBelieve

That particular to-do list, taped to our Bible, placed on the mirror where we shave, fastened to the dash of the car, wherever it is can truly help us through any kind of a day we may be facing. Personally, I'd add an 8th item on that to-do list:

"Thank God for today, and for who I am."

If the first to-do list we deal with each day were something like that one, wouldn't dealing with any other lists be made just a bit easier?

Bottom Line Thought: How could your days be changed by first focusing on your spiritual to-do list? How could that affect the way you relate to others throughout the day?

Day 101:
Every.Single.Day !!

There are 365 days in a year. We all know that don't we? One day follows another, and another, and so on, and before we know it we're at year's end. Then, we start another cycle.

I don't believe in coincidences, but sometimes I feel compelled to believe in what I call Godcidences. The following tidbit of information is one of those times:

The phrase "do not be afraid" is written in the Bible 365 times."

Might we consider that there may some divine connection between that often repeated statement and the number of days in the year?

What are some of the things we find ourselves being afraid of?

- We fear the unknown, e.g. what might result from a decision we make.
- We fear ourselves at times because we know our weaknesses.
- We fear the future because we don't know what lies ahead.
- We fear a path we should follow because we don't know where it leads.
- And, there are many more.

Isn't the opposite of fear, trust? Since almost all of our *real* fears have to do with matters that will affect our lives in one way or another, perhaps we really need to zero in on those 365 "do not be afraid" biblical mentions. How best to accomplish that than by recognizing that when it comes to our lives, God has a plan, and it is our job to trust Him.

Yes, perhaps that phrase was on purpose, to teach us that we can rely on Him, and trust Him, and not be afraid. EVERY.SINGLE.DAY!

Bottom Line Thought: If you were to look deep within yourself, would you find that there are times when you fear needlessly when you should be placing your trust in God? Could one reason for that be because you think your plan for your life might be better than His plan?

Day 102:
Our Words

What would it be like if we couldn't talk? I know that if I couldn't talk I wouldn't have to eat my words at times, I wouldn't have to apologize for saying the wrong things so often, and I wouldn't be able to blurt out stupid stuff at the most inopportune moments. While a lot of good things can and do come out of our mouths, it's the inappropriate stuff that gets us in trouble, because it's those words that;

- Hurt, sting, bite, and burn others
- Build barriers and tear down bridges in relationships
- Tell more about us, who we really are, and what we are because of the damage they do.

If the only words that came from our mouths were a result of Godly thought, we would find that they

- Build others up
- Help us construct bridges in broken relationships
- Comfort those in need and provide joy and calm to the restless
- Tell a lot about us, who we really are, and what we are because they are Godly.

Our words are a reflection of our hearts and minds. Whether engaged in conversation, discussion, or an argument, we need to <u>take the time to taste our words before we spit them out.</u> There is an old Sufi saying that addresses that. *"Before you speak, let your words pass through 3 gates. At the first gate, ask yourself 'Is it true?', At the second, ask yourself 'Is it necessary?'. At the third gate, ask "Is it kind.'"*

If we can talk, it will help a lot if we talk to God about the problems our words cause. He had a way with words you know.

Bottom Line Thought: Do you find that some of your words are like daggers? Have you been hurt by the words of others? How did you react? Do you need to consider a new approach to talking?

Day 103:
Fish Swimming Upstream

Life's a beast sometimes. We feel like a fish swimming upstream. Salmon are well known for that practice on an annual basis. I've had the pleasure of seeing that phenomenon of nature in Alaska. During the spawning season hundreds of thousands of salmon struggle to make their way upstream in the rivers and streams that dump into the ocean waterways. While on that journey they

- Fight and clamor for space
- Struggle mightily to find their way up ever narrowing streams
- Are prey for fishermen and wildlife looking for an easy catch while making their way
- Face a multitude of obstacles such as rocks, ledges, blockages, crowded pooling spots and shallow waters
- Tire drastically due to the constant fight against the rushing water and obstacles—*but they never stop their journey.*

The spawning process is instinctive to the salmon, and their focus never wavers. It is a natural part of their being to complete their journey to the spawning areas.

In our hearts, don't we as humans have inborn natural instincts as well? Our need to survive is certainly the one most often named. Another is our need to follow goodness and reject evil in our lives. For many of us, the goodness instinct is a belief in God and a desire to follow Jesus. At times in our Christian lives that instinct brings us times when we feel that we, just like the salmon, are swimming upstream against any number of obstacles. Yet, despite those obstacles, we keep focused on the journey. Sometimes we just have to remind ourselves that we don't care what's in the way, we're going to make that swim, and we're going to make it successfully, in spite of the obstacles.

Bottom Line Thought: Nature offers us many analogies we can apply to our daily lives, such as the phenomenon of the annual salmon run. Can you find any that apply to your daily life and walk as a Christian?

Day 104:
Surprise!

We like nice surprises don't we? A nice surprise such as a random act of kindness directed our way, an unexpected affirmation, a smile or kind word from a stranger each goes a long way to making our day a better day. We also get a kick out of doing something nice as a surprise for someone else. We think those surprises make for a happy person.

Unfortunately, there are surprises that aren't nice, like when we hear of the sudden death of a loved one or a friend. Death is sad at any time, but at least we can somewhat prepare ourselves for a death when we know, or have been told, that it is expected.

The truth is, none of us know when our own death will come, do we? We don't know when our last goodbye will be spoken, or under what circumstances. Isn't that a strong incentive for us to live our lives continually striving to be men who follow Christ?

The only surprise any of us should really crave is the one that comes when we die and we find heaven is so much more than we ever imagined it to be.

Bottom Line Thought: Are you conducting your life in such a way that there will be no surprise about where you are going when you die? The only surprise should be that it will be much better than you ever dreamed about.

Day 105:
And In This Corner...

I'll date myself here. When I was a kid we used to watch the Friday Night Fights on our 1st television, one with a huge wooden cabinet and a tiny 9" black and white screen. The ring announcer would introduce each of the fighters by pointing to a corner and saying "and in this corner"....naming who the boxer was. After the announcements, the boxers would have at it, beating on each other.

Life gets to be like a boxing match sometimes doesn't it? There are times when we feel we are getting the crud beat out of us, or we feel like we are someone's personal punching bag. There are times when we know we are doing right, yet we get clobbered again and again. We punch back, and yet our adversary, who or whatever it is seems to have the upper hand against us. It is those times that can cause our faith to weaken isn't it?

One of the realities that many of us became acutely aware of as we embarked on our spiritual journeys was that we were ambushed by God's grace and love in a big way. And in discovering that, we found that *as long as we know that God is for us, it doesn't matter who is against us.*

Perhaps, when life gets tough, we need to picture ourselves as a fighter in a boxing ring. Our name is called, and then we hear "and in this corner is God." At that point we can drop our gloves and simply go into a clinch with Him to get us through the fight.

Bottom Line Thought: You don't have to be going through the fight of your life to clinch God do you? He's there for you in every little battle isn't he? How often do you turn away from the fight to embrace Him?

Day 106:
Frienemies (fren-uh-mees)

Many of us enjoy NASCAR racing. A source of enjoyment for me is listening to one of the network announcers, Darrell Waltrip, himself a former racer. He's good at coining words (Darrell-isms, as I call them). One such word is "frienemies." The word describes drivers racing on one of the super speedways, where drafting is a necessity, right up to the last lap or two. Briefly, it means all of the drivers are friends during most of the race where they need each other as drafting partners to keep up with the pack. However, within the last few laps, because of the desire of each to win the race, they become enemies, though they still need each other to help them get near the finish line.

In our lives we all have friends. We need friends because we are basically social beings. We, who are on a spiritual journey, often have some very special friends who mentor us or help us through some of the rough spots that life brings us. They are the ones who will hold us accountable for our actions, to help us stay the course.

Most of us don't have enemies in our lives. Because of our walk with Christ, we are forgiving and understanding of the behaviors and character blemishes of others because we have been there. We know that when we were there, someone(s) took the time and made the effort to help us change so that we would have a finish line to race toward.

As Christians, we have been reminded many times of the example of Jesus...to love our enemies. In NASCAR terms, that tells us to make frienemies as we race on this super speedway of life toward the finish line. We need them so that our light might shine and they need us so that they can see our light. Everybody wins in this race.

Bottom Line Thought: So, let's say there is someone in your life that you really don't like—at all. You may think of that person as an enemy. If you are really walking with the Lord, how can you change so that that person will become a frienemy so they may see your light?

Day 107

Healing Wanted

A quote attributed to Ronald Reagan is, *"The time has come to turn to God and reassert our trust in Him for the healing of America. Our country is in need of and ready for a spiritual renewal."*

Regardless of our political beliefs, most of us will agree with that statement. We are, in present times, witnessing attack upon attack of the moral and spiritual fiber of America and the people within it. Evil forces and spiritual warfare are strongly attacking individuals and the principals upon which this country was founded.

If each of us, as men, commit to being better men, husbands, and fathers, this country can grow in spiritual strength. This will be influenced by the Christ like decisions and choices we make as we individually take the time and effort needed to change our own lives, and then allow our light to shine on others.

Spiritual renewal is a one by one, person to person process. The whole of America is the sum of its parts—us.

Bottom Line Thought: Will you do your part? Will you share what God has done in your life with others? Will you share the experiences you have learned in this book with others to help them grow spiritually?

Day 108:
What About The Kids?

"Our kids are the future of the world." One implication of that saying is that it is *we* who are *raising* the future of the world. Here are some observations I've made over the past couple of decades that makes for a scary thought;

- More young kids are being shuffled off to pre-school or sitters because both parents work, and there are less and less stay at home parents.
- Television (the one-eyed god) and electronics have damaged social interaction skills in the youth.
- Social media and cell phones have become must-haves for children.
- Less and less kids seem to play outdoors.
- PTA/PTC groups are clamoring for parental involvement.
- The agenda for public education is becoming more and more liberal.
- Childhood is being robbed because parents are willing to let their kids grow up way too soon and are too busy to play like kids with them.
- Many parents are not bringing up their children with a spiritual world view.

We can all understand that at times families face financial challenges that demand that both parents work. If those challenges are because the family has succumbed to the "monster of more," then perhaps the spiritual fabric of the family is torn or worn. Abdicating parental obligations in favor of worldly stuff is not conducive to raising our kids with a spiritual worldview.

If we don't teach our children how to follow Christ,
the world will teach them not to.

That statement brings to mind several points: 1) How much about the Christian walk will kids learn from television, social media, and texting? 2) If our children are so important, why is it that so much of their upbringing is placed in the hands of others?

Some, like me, have raised our children while we were non-believers. That doesn't mean they all turned out bad, but in my case only a couple have chosen a Christ like walk for their lives, and those of their children—something that is very, very sad.

Bottom Line Thought: Can you accept the fact that it is never too late to change, no matter where you are in your spiritual walk? Are you preparing your children for a Christian walk? How important are they to you?

Day 109:
Good Enough

I worked in and around the construction business during parts of my life. I found that there are basically two types of workers—those who say "that's good enough", and those who want to do it right. The "good enoughers" tend to cut corners when there is a good chance it won't be caught by someone and have to be done over again. They are gambling on their lack of perfection.

Sometimes in our spiritual journeys as men, we come under scrutiny that is uncomfortable to us. We are humans who, try as we might, still make mistakes, still fall short in our walk, and still show signs of our brokenness. We will swear when we don't want to, behave stupidly, or do dumb things without too much thought beforehand. At those times it easy to feel the vibes that we are not "good enough" because someone around us may seem openly pious or enjoys being vocally judgmental. I'm not talking about accountability here, where iron sharpens iron, but rather those folks in our lives who genuinely view us, flawed as we are, as never being "good enough."

Do we answer to God, or do we answer to men? Isn't our journey one of constantly trying and striving to live up to God's standards while being comfortable in the knowledge of His grace for all failures? Or, is our journey all about living up to the standards of folks who have taken as their job the judgment of those who will fail in some way? That's all of us, by the way.

God knows us and He knows that we aren't now, nor ever will be "good enough", and yet He has promised that there will be a place for us as long as we believe and strive to do the job of living with Christ.

There comes a point when we have to realize that we'll never be good enough for some people. The question is, is that our problem, or theirs?

As long as we never say "that's good enough" about our spiritual growth job, we'll always have the Big Guy in our corner, and He's the one who really matters—not those others.

Bottom Line Thought: Trying to be good enough for the benefit of someone else is not healthy. Do you ever get overly concerned about what others may think of you?

Day 110:
Ordinary

Aren't we all just ordinary people living ordinary lives? Regardless of our race, creed, background, or socio-economic status, we are all just ordinary people. We are all covered in skin, we bleed red, and we put our pants on one leg at a time. What makes us think some may not be just as ordinary is because they do some extraordinary things in their lives. At our base root, *we were all*, even those who do extraordinary things, made in God's image, which makes us all ordinary. Ordinary men do extraordinary things.

Jesus, and later the Apostles and disciples, were all ordinary men, but they had extraordinary abilities, gifts, and lives. They did extraordinary things because they had courage. In their time, they found it took courage to be ordinary. By being ordinary, they spread the Word among other ordinary men.

In today's times, it takes no less courage to be ordinary. It is that courage which frees us to be bold and faithful in our efforts to be Christ following men. Our pastors and the leaders of our churches are just like us—ordinary. They use their gifts and talents to shepherd us, just as we use our courage and abilities to disciple others to bring them to a life in Christ. The only thing that can stop us from being ordinary is fear.

Bottom Line Thought: Have you embraced your ordinariness? Can you be comfortable with it? Do you have the courage it takes as an ordinary man to use your special talents and ability to further the Kingdom work in your daily life?

Day 111:
Happiness

What is happiness? Loosely put, it is the state of being happy, or, a state of contentment or well-being. We have heard that money can't buy happiness, yet many of us, through our actions, don't really believe that do we? We buy a new car, tool, or toy and initially we "feel" happy because we have something new. That sense of being happy over our newly acquired object eventually wears off doesn't it?

Why do we sometimes think of ourselves as unhappy? Why do some folks seem to be terminally unhappy—those folks we really don't like to be around for very long? Isn't it because we, or they, can't find contentment or a sense of well-being at that point in time? We do know that happiness isn't something we can't go to Wal-Mart and buy don't we?

One of the easiest ways to find happiness, not the temporary kind that comes from buying something new, but the more lasting and meaningful kind, is to simply look within ourselves and look at the good we see there. We need to set our temporary issues and problems aside and recognize that there is a lot of good residing there under our skin.

If we need to double down a bit, because we may not be sure we have anything to be happy about, we need only look around us and we will find others who are far less fortunate than we are, folks who have stuff happening to them that we wouldn't wish on our worse enemy. And, often times as we look at those folks we will find that they too have a sense of contentment and well-being because their particular issues aren't worse than they are.

Being happy is infectious to those around us. Granted, there are some grouches out there that may find our happiness annoying, and there may be some who are terminally unhappy. What *we don't know* is if our happiness could be an example for them.

God didn't make us to be unhappy. He made us to be content, content with ourselves and what is going on around us. As long as we trust Him, he will take care of our well-being.

Bottom Line Thought: Are you a happy person generally? Do you feel contentment in your life no matter what is going on?

Day 112:
Stale Bread And Crackers

Sometimes our relationships or marriages are like bread or saltine crackers that have been opened and not resealed properly—stale. That doesn't mean they are necessarily bad. It means they just don't have the freshness they once had.

What do we do with our stale bread and crackers? Typically, don't we throw it out or feed it to the birds and squirrels? We can't do that when our relationship or marriage goes stale can we? That being the case, what do we do?

Regardless of who we think may be at fault for a stale marriage, we really only have one option—start by changing ourselves by;

- Looking within for ways we have left the wrapper open to staleness.
- Reaffirming our love in new ways, and doing so more often.
- Placing the value on the marriage or relationship that it should have.
- Not taking the other party for granted.
- Expressing ourselves as a committed partner.
- Committing to a no-fail mentality about it.

We need to believe in our heart of hearts that it is possible to fall in love, not just once when we found the one we are committed to, but that we can each and every day of our lives with them. If we do that, we, and they, will never get stale. If we do that, it will become a partnership of amazement, because they will follow your example.

Bottom Line Thought: Stretch your thinking to include this about you: "I never thought it was possible to fall in love with her over and over and over again." PS: Has God ever stopped loving you?

Day 113:

How Hard Is It?

Some of us make kindness a selective thing don't we? We appreciate it when someone is kind to us, particularly when there seems to be no real reason for it. Yet, we aren't always as kind as we wish we would be—like when;

- We know someone who is financially struggling, yet we don't help because we are too concerned about parting with some of our money.
- We see the homeless person on the street approaching us and we avoid eye contact or make a quick turn away.
- We know the elderly lady across the street has trouble getting about, yet we conveniently ignore her plight, leaving it to her kids or relatives to help.
- We know one of the guys in our small group is really struggling yet we don't find the time to give him our shoulder to lean on.
- We think random acts of kindness are for sissies and women.

Kindness breeds kindness, no matter what station of life the giver or receiver is at. Kindness, particularly when unexpected and random in nature, is a true form of humility. Kindness with no limits on race, creed, need, or socio-economic status is the ultimate in kindness. Jesus, throughout His ministry provided us with example after example of the most humble and basic forms of kindness—because He loved all.

Bottom Line Thought: How hard can it be for you to live a life of humble kindness with no expectation for a return?

Day 114:
Making Change

"Oh, he'll never change"

"I can't change; I'm too old for that."

"Some things never change."

"Change is so hard."

Those are things we utter once in a while, right? I've done it, especially at times when the change needed is about me. That's making an excuse isn't it, or it's buying into a lie. What we are saying is different than what we really mean;

- We are comfortable with the "known" and we fear the results of change.
- We are basically lazy and complacent about ourselves.
- We worry about what others might think about us.
- We don't trust ourselves to be able to follow through.
- We look at what needs changing as a habit (and it may be), and we think habits can't be changed.
- We haven't fully placed our trust in God to help us make that change.

"Changing our lives is a process, not an event."

Surgery changes and fixes something, it's an event. Changing the sheets on a bed is an event. Changing a radio station in our car is an event. Growing up was a process for us, certainly not an event. Changing our lives to make it better is a process.

Anything in our lives that stands in the way of our living as Christ like men can be changed—*if we want it to*. Making that change is only a result of our wanting to do so, choosing to do it, and then doing it. We're not talking about change for a dollar here. We're talking about life change. It's process versus event. God is always patient with those wanting to change.

Bottom Line Thought: Are there areas in your life that you think need changing? If you asked your wife and kids, how would they answer that? What is God whispering to you about change? Are your answers in sync with what He would say?

Day 115:
Go Ahead And Do It

There are times in our lives when we get overwhelmed with joy aren't there? One of those moments is the births of our children. Another might be when we feared the worst of a medical condition, but received the doctor's assurance that it wasn't as bad as it first seemed. Or, maybe we received an unexpected promotion when we had absolutely no idea it was pending. It's at times like those when we may have thought to ourselves one of the following;

"That right there was a God thing"

"I just had a Jesus moment"

"God's handprint was all over that"

"Thank you Jesus!"

At those times don't we feel a little bit giddy? We know that whatever it was, it was a special moment, something a result of anything far greater than ourselves. We look at that instant with a sense of awe and joy.

Maybe we let ourselves get into too much of a rut to see all of the times in our daily lives that can offer us the same amount of joy and awe. Perhaps we get too focused on the big picture to look at all of the wonderful paint strokes that make up that picture. And, sadly, maybe we are just too up-tight to let some giddiness out.

What impact would it have on our outlook, on the lives of those around us, and in the lives of others if we actually looked for, and actively sought out, those special Jesus moments that are always around us? What is there to stop us?

Bottom Line Thought: Go ahead and do it. Find something to make you stop, look up, smile, and say, "I know that was you God! Thanks!" You'll have a happier day because of it.

Day 116:
What's The Point?

Church signs, the ones where the message gets changed regularly, are sometimes quite funny, yet the short message packs a punch for those that read them. One such sign recently read;

"Life without God is like an unsharpened pencil. No point."

Whoever worded the sign made a point. An unsharpened pencil can't be used.

Bottom Line Thought: Are you a pencil in God's hand? Can you be used by Him to draw others to Him? If not, what's the point of your life?

Day 117:
Living The Good Life

There are terms we use facetiously. One we use happens when someone asks us how we're doing and we spit out "living the good life." We know we are ordinary blue collar folks with bills, kids, schedules to juggle, work to be concerned about, but we try to put a positive spin on it all. It beats using the time worn "I'm fine," which most of recognize as a polite, yet maybe not completely true, response.

Many of us probably think of the "good life" as one where there is enough money to make ends meet and have some left over, where we are worry free and with few problems. That's just not the live of the average Joe though, is it?

Actually, there are many men living the good life. Those are the men who are striving daily to live their lives as Christ followers. They are the men who know, that in spite of any earthly issues they may be dealing with, they are building their lives for the future, a future in eternity. To them, with Christ at the center of their lives, they are living the good life.

"A good life is when you assume nothing, do more, need less, smile often, dream big, laugh a lot, and realize how blessed you are" is a saying from an unknown source that pretty much captures what the good life is.

As long as we continue to trust God through each and every issue, problem, hardship, concern and doubt, we don't have to fear anything. When we have a life without fear, we are living the good life.

Bottom Line Thought: Do you just say you are living the good life, or are you actually living it?

Day 118:
America

HOW MANY OF US ARE LIVING OUR LIVES IN SUCH A WAY AS TO PUT THE "B" BACK IN IT?

Bottom Line Thought: Our kids are the future. Are you raising yours in such a manner that the moral fabric of our country will not suffer any further?

Day 119:
Boldness

"He took a bold leap when he changed jobs"

"He put up a bold fight with the disease that was ravaging him"

"He was bold to stand up to his boss that way."

"It took boldness to walk away from that."

Don't we generally think of boldness as a macho thing? By doing so maybe we're limiting ourselves a bit. Real boldness is listening to our gut, heart, and God's leading, and acting on it when everything else is telling us to stay away from the situation.

Here's a story to explain that; years ago, a man was walking in total darkness. Some would consider him a nice guy, but his life was ruled by sin. He was all but godless. A young man who he barely knew approached him one day, and to make a long story short, led him to Christ during lunch. That young man was bold. Years later, when the man had fallen away from his faith and resumed his life on the dark side, his daughter stepped out of her comfort zone and paved the way for the man to return to a life of faith. She too was bold, because she was concerned that by stepping out her father would reject her.

Us men aren't always as bold as we think we are, nor, perhaps, as bold as we want to be. It takes boldness to be the father that will provide a tough love discipline in a godly manner for his children when the peer pressure they face is much against that. It takes boldness to continue to keep the faith when we are getting the crap beat out of us on all fronts of our worldly life. It takes boldness to challenge another man when we see that his spiritual life is in need of help. It takes boldness to speak up for the good and just when we witness unfair and unjust treatment of another. And it takes boldness to relentlessly carry the message of Jesus to others—especially those we don't know.

Bottom Line Thought: How is your boldness meter? Does it get off kilter from fear? Be bold, my friend—someone's life may depend on it. Mine did a couple of times.

Day 120:
Just One

> We all have two lives.
>
> The second one starts when we realize we only have one.
>
> Tom Hiddleston
Source unknown

The above statement nails it for a lot of guys doesn't it? Sometimes we live like we have two lives—our everyday lives where we work, play, raise a family, and get in a bit of R & R. We say to ourselves, "I'll get around to that other stuff later on." We're talking about our spiritual lives. We'll get to that when things slow down, when the kids are gone, when I've climbed up the company ladder, etc. "I'll get that later." Fortunately, sometimes we get a wakeup call.

How does the wake up occur? Maybe we have just watched a close friend who is our age die suddenly, leaving a family with small kids behind. Perhaps we have just found out we have (gasp) a heart condition that calls for us to slow down. It could even happen when the family rebels, when you realize that they just don't seem to revere you as much as they once did or the wife is threatening to leave you. Maybe it happens at the exact moment you realize you are taking your last breath. Oops, it's too late now.

Our second life, our real life, begins when we know in that empty pit in our heart that something is missing—something eternal. It comes when we realize that that hole can only be filled by becoming a new man, a spiritual man, a man who knows Jesus. It begins when we realize what our true priorities are, as we realize the duplicity and fruitfulness of everything else we have been chasing. It begins when we choose to be godly men.

Yes, we do have two lives. One we waste. One we cherish. One works against us. One works for us. One makes us successful. One makes us successful men. One pleases us. One pleases God. Real men have just one life. Pick which is yours.

Bottom Line Thought: Have you reached the crossroads where you pick one life or the other? If you're going to be real about your life, you can only have one. Which choice will you make?

Day 121:
Real Friends Are Real

When I was on the dark side of life and had money, I spent a lot of time in bars and I had a lot of "friends." When I was out and about and doing some shady and illegal things, I had a lot of "friends." When I was in high school and hanging out with the wrong crowd, I had a lot of "friends." Over time, I changed, was brought to the Light, and you know what—none of those "friends" ever looked me up to see how I was doing, if I was okay.

It's been said that in our lifetimes we are fortunate if we can count the number of true friends on one hand. I'm inclined to believe that. Today, as I was taking the dog on one of his fertilizing missions I thought about the subject of friends. It was clear to me that there are real friends, and there are "friends" who are just people we know or have known. Those "friends";

- Are great at feeding your ego as a macho man.
- Don't really care about you, but what you bring to the table.
- Have little genuine feeling about anything, them and you included.
- May not have a healthy outlook of people of the opposite sex.
- Are "in it" for themselves more often than not.

Once out of the dark, and as I started to develop a whole new past steeped in spiritual and Christian values, I discovered a whole new side to friends—real friends;

- They love me unconditionally, warts and all.
- They care more for me than I may ever realize.
- They share their emotions and feelings and help me release mine.
- They have a healthy outlook on sex matters.
- They are "in it" all the way--for me.

Friends like that will walk the walk with each of us, through all of our struggles and temptations. They will call our stuff when it's needed, to hold us accountable. They won't direct our lives, but they will walk every step with us as we walk our walk, and point out the trouble spots so we can make the choice. They are few and far between, but they are loyal beyond what we are used to. We call them brothers.

Bottom Line Thought: Do you have at least one good real friend? Why not? Can you be that special friend to someone? Why not?

Day 122:
Liberal Logic

Does that meme bother you? The message it conveys bothered me, as I imagine it does a lot of us. The senseless truth of the message is a morality issue, one facing the nation today. It is but one issue that has diminished the morality of our country, one among many which is threatening the spiritual and moral fabric of this nation.

Why is this happening? I will offer that complacency on the part of many of us is one of the causes. We have allowed ourselves to become numbed by a progression of morality watering down events of many years, starting with the removal of scripture reading in the classrooms in 1963 as a result of a Supreme Court ruling in favor of Madalyn Murray O'hare, the atheist activist. In many ways we have "caved in", saying "oh well, what can I do about it?"

Complacency (apathy) is a form of a soul and heart wrecking cancer. It grows slowly and steadily, robbing us of our spiritual vibrancy. One of the results is 15 year old girls being allowed to get abortions without their parents consent, even though they have to get their parents' permission to take aspirin at school. It's upside down isn't it?

What can we, as parents, do? The first thing is to realize that if you roll over, you have rolled over—you have given up. That is complacency. Here are some suggestions:

- Dare to be different. Get angry and vocal about such issues.
- Get <u>actively</u> indignant about issues that are spiritually and morally wrong.
- Don't keep it inside. Share your feelings and beliefs with others.
- Pray for "sane" leadership and actively seek and promote morally sound candidates for local offices. Strong politics always starts at the bottom levels.
- Insist that your family not "cave in", talk about the issues from a spiritual context.
- Wear your values on your sleeves. Does it really matter what others think?

It is really all about <u>taking personal responsibility</u>. It becomes a one by one, by one, process of people having enough, of people getting angry about moral issues.

Bottom Line Thought: If your 15 year old daughter came home to tell you she had had an abortion without your knowledge, would that be okay with you?

Day 123:
Public Enemy # 1

"I don't have an enemy in the world" How many times have we heard that? Maybe we're all the same. We really don't have any enemies out there. Oh, there may be some that don't particularly like us, but enemies—nope, they're not there. Well, there is just one in my case, and perhaps yours. My enemy is me. At times he's just as bad as public enemy #1, the one we see pictures of in the post office.

The enemy within me is the one that doesn't like me. He pokes his head up every once in a while to remind me that I'm not as good a person as I think I am. He's the one that tries to dictate and direct my bad behavior, the one who will try to tear me down in a heartbeat. He shows up in different forms, like;

- Anger, or pouting and withdrawal, when something doesn't go my way.
- Retaliation or sarcasm when I think someone is trying to best me.
- The indignant and self righteous me when a hurt wasn't really meant.
- Sarcasm when I know I'm right and someone else isn't.
- Smart mouthing when I am trying to put someone else down.

The enemy within is the one who doesn't want me to be forgiving, but expects full forgiveness for every slight, real or imagined. He's the one who doesn't want to look at the others viewpoint, even though it might be solid, valid, and truthful. He'll throw words out of my mouth faster than Clint Eastwood's .41 Magnum, with the same amount of impact.

The bottom line is that the enemy within is the one that fires up my "conclusion gland"—the one that has a hard time drawing a right conclusion about someone or something. He also has very good aim. I've proven I can shoot myself in the foot time after time.

Our relationship with God helps put the cuffs on public enemy #1. Through God we learn forgiveness. We forgive ourselves, he forgives us, and we forgive others. We experience forgiveness asked for, forgiveness graciously received, and self forgiveness through which we can learn. Yep, public enemy #1 is slowly realizing he can't bully me around anymore.

Bottom Line Thought: Is there a public enemy # 1 in your life? Do you share all of his antics in prayer with the Lord, and ask for strength?

Day 124:
Evil Will Not Win

Since time began bad things have happened to good people. In recent times there have been many that have captured the nation because of their inherent evil;

- The 9-11 Twin Towers destruction by airplanes
- The Columbine shootings in Colorado
- The movie theater shootings, also in Colorado
- The Sandy Hook massacre
- The Boston Marathon bombing

Often many will ask after such incidents, "How can God let something like this happen?", or "If God is so good, why does He let such things happen?" Many books have been written which try to answer those very questions. People want to know why bad things happen to good people.

I'm just a blue collar guy with no extensive education, particularly of a biblical or spiritual nature. But, never in any of my reading have I ever found anything to suggest that God stops all evil. I don't think there would be very many of us who wouldn't call any of the above events anything but evil based. I personally think evil based events like the above are a test of our individual resolve. Will they shake our faith in the Lord, or won't they?

I do know this—based on the fact that history always seems to repeat itself;

1. Tragic events of a horrific nature will always occur sometime as long as there are people.
2. There are always some purely evil people in the world.
3. No legal or preventative measures will ever stop evil events from happening or evil people from doing them.
4. Evil nature in mankind cannot be legislated or controlled by mankind.

Whenever evil such as the above occurs we really have only one clear choice to make:

We can overcome evil, or we will let evil win.

By cowering in the face of evil, it wins. By our standing tall and believing that God is mightier than all evil in the world, evil will not win.

Bottom Line Thought: Do horrific and major evil events shake your faith in God? Do you start to question your faith in those times?

Day 125:

50-20 Vision

Do we really like the people we have become? Are we the person we had hoped we would be, the one we envisioned in those times years ago when we thought about the hopes and dreams for our future? Did the road of real life fail to connect with the road of fantasy? Real life has a way of having real roadblocks we have to navigate around, while fantasy life has easily removable roadblocks.

One of the roadblocks in real life is our "preventer of real life" gene. It's called our obsession with our past. Don't we have a tendency to carry around all of our stuff (our life junk) and relive it over and over again? Regarding our past, our "rememberers" work very, very well, while our "forgetterers" don't work. How do we get past that roadblock? Accept this about our past;

"Our past isn't our past if it still impacts our present.

An appropriate quote attributed to Martin Luther King applies: "If your head is made of butter, don't sit near the fire." Not releasing our past is closely akin to Mr. Butterhead sitting by that fire. It will not go away, rather it will just continue to melt and make a mess of things.

It is never too late to become who we envisioned ourselves to be—never. Dump the junk. Put it right into God's hands. And then trust Him to deal with it. He's got huge hands. He can handle it all. Then we can put all of our energy into seeing the long view of life through 50-20 vision. It takes much less energy to see with that 50-20 vision than it does to deal with old junk. It's a win-win!

Bottom Line Thought: How's your vision? Are you looking forward with 50-20 vision for the long view, or are you still seeing junk with your 20-20 vision?

Day 126:
The Train

At birth, each of us boarded a train where we met our parents. We believed that they would always be traveling with us. However, along the way, at some station, our parents stepped down from the train, leaving us to continue our journey alone. As time went by, at different stations, others boarded the train. Many of these became significant to us. Brothers, sisters, friends, the love of our life, and even children boarded the train.

As time goes on, many of those will step down from the train at different stations. Some, by getting off the train, will leave a permanent vacuum. Others will go so unnoticed that we won't realize that they are gone, their seats now empty.

This train ride will be a mixed bag of joy, sorrow, expectations, hellos, surprises, great happiness, ravaging hurts, and great happenings, lost dreams, missed opportunities, farewells and goodbyes. The trip will be successful if we have a good relationship with all that board the train while we are on it—including the Engineer who actually owns the train. In fact, in the Engineer's Book it clearly states that while on the train, each is to give the best of themselves and trust that the Engineer will provide for them a safe and rewarding trip.

There is a mystery about the train. No one knows at which station he/she will step down from the train. And that is why, in the Engineer's Book he shares with all of his passengers, he shows each passenger how to live the best way—love, forgive, and offer the best of who you are. It is important that each passenger do this, because when the time comes for us to step down and leave our seat empty, we will be prepared to go to that very special train station where the Engineer lives—Heaven.

Bottom Line Thought: I hope that when I get to the station when it is my time to get off the train, that I will have lived in a manner that is consistent with the Engineer's book, and will have been some sort of an example for those still on the train. How about you?

Day 127:
Reactions

I had a friend, 10 years older than me, who I knew for a long time. We'd golf together, dine together, then get royally drunk together until the bar kicked us out. The ban never lasted long, because we spent a lot of money at the place, and we were "people of position" (hah!). Then came the point in time when we'd golf—but he'd go home to eat and spend the evening at home. Some years passed, until one night I came home drunk and couldn't stand myself living like that anymore so I instinctively called that friend to come get me because I was sure I was going crazy. He did, and he took me to his place to talk and have coffee. That was when I found out he had stopped drinking and started living. That was the early turning point in my life.

In ensuing years, our relationship as a couple of guys living a sober life became very special. He willingly shared a lot of wisdom about life with me. One of the things he shared was about reactions and their effect on relationships. He shared that when he was drunk, his wife knew where all the buttons were, and she would push them unmercifully, and he would react—usually in an inappropriate manner. With sobriety, he found that by not reacting inappropriately when his buttons were pushed, the marriage improved, and the times that the buttons were used diminished. One of the things he shared was, "I found out that when I react in a bad way, it is like sticking a knife in the heart of our relationship—and the heart gets damaged."

We don't have to be drunks to react in a bad way when we are in less than pleasant discussions do we? Yet, don't we often do that—perhaps because we think that we will somehow get an upper hand by doing so? Even during the course of a perfectly normal conversation we can get offended erroneously because we take something we hear personally, when that intent was never present. And if we react in a way we shouldn't, even if it feels natural to us, aren't we really just sticking a knife into the heart of the relationship? Reactions can be relationship killers or relationship healers. We have a choice of which type to use.

Bottom Line Thought: Have you gauged how your reactions affect your relationship?

Day 128:
We're Gardeners

Wildflowers and weeds grow freely, fast, and without any care. We need only to look at our yards and lawns to see that. Whether the seeds land by the wind or are dropped by the birds, once they hit soil, they grow without any care. Our gardens and flower beds are different. We plant the seeds, we water and feed them, and we care for them as they grow into beauty and usefulness.

Some of us, however, don't have green thumbs, and we leave the lawns, gardens and flower beds to others. But, as men of faith, *we are all spiritual gardeners.*

- Our garden plot lies within the hearts and minds of those around us—our family, friends, co-workers, strangers.
- Our seeds are the words, actions, and deeds we say and do around those people in our lives.
- Our gardening tools are the Word, the example we consistently set, and our obvious love for the Lord.
- Our fertilizer is our passion, love for others, patience, and gentleness we use in growing the seeds we have planted.

Christ chose 12 very ordinary, and in some cases quite jaded, men to be His gardeners among all men during His life and after His death. Their job was to plant, care for, and grow the seeds of Christianity. Their garden plot—the world. The obvious irony of what He did when He selected those men was that they were just like us—ordinary. In some cases they were troubled, and some were far from the nicest of men before He planted the seed in them.

We don't have to be anything special to be a Gardner for God. We don't have to have unblemished pasts, nor do we have to live the perfect life—because we can't. We just have to have the desire to keep growing ourselves as we use all that is available to us as gardeners to spread His word among men—one, by one, by one. Our gardening is simply a people to people thing.

Bottom Line Thought: So, Johnny Appleseed, are you working in the Garden for God?

Day 129:
Straight Arrow

"He's a straight arrow." We've heard that before, yes? Whenever we hear someone called that, we believe him to be a straight shooter, not a liar or cheat, and a man who stays true to the course.

An arrow that is bent cannot be shot with good accuracy. They must be straight, to an exacting degree, to consistently hit the target. But, it's not just the arrow that makes that happen. An archer or hunter is involved, and in order for the shot to hit its mark, he must pull the arrow back deliberately and straight, all the while carefully aiming and focusing on the target. The better his focus and aim, the greater will be his opportunity for a great shot.

We are all born with just one shot at life before we die. One shot, that's it. Some of us have had do-over's. Those do-over's are Gods way of letting us refocus and aim once again—but we're still on that one and only shot we have at life.

We are, therefore, both the arrow and the archer. When we are straight arrows we are assured that we will reach our target—Heaven, and as the archers we are responsible for the aim and focus needed to do that. As the archer, we compensate for any dents and flaws on the imperfect arrows we are as humans.

Bottom Line Thought: Have you considered the thought that you have just the one shot at life? Are you a straight arrow to your family, friends, strangers you meet, and God?

Day 130:
Stress

If we were to ask any of our friends or family members who have had strokes, overly high blood pressure, eating or sleeping disorders, or heart attacks what might be a contributing factor, almost universally we would hear, stress. Doctors have singled that cause out for a number of health issues we face.

I'm no doctor, and thus I can't get into a medical discussion about stress, but from my own experience this is what I know about it;

- Stress is what I feel as a result of worrying or fretting about things I have no control over, to the point that it affects my attitude, behavior, and my well-being. In doing so, it also affects my relationships with others around me. It drives a wedge into my spiritual foundation. It is self inflicted, and it is not communicable.

There are medications that are prescribed to control stress. A change in dietary habits also goes a long way in controlling it. A change in lifestyle can not only relieve stress, but prevent it. No, we're not talking the "be happy—don't worry" thing here.

The most solid thing I know of to prevent a reoccurrence of stress once we have it under control is faith. Stress affects our heads and hearts. Faith lives in our heads and hearts if we choose it. If we have truly strong faith, we may minimize our stress because we fully trust the Lord with our lives, not ourselves. Think of it this way—we get stress from things that *we do to ourselves—nowhere else*. By the way, we can't buy faith at Walgreens. We have to find it on our own.

My way=Stress

His way=Faith=No stress

Faith, *in combination with* a change in our lifestyle, will give us our best shot at controlling our stress. It's something many of us want to ignore, simply because we have a human tendency to want it now and not fully trusting God with our lives.

Bottom Line Thought: Only a simple choice remains. Which will it be, stress or faith?

Day 131:
The Hard Question

Case 1: A healthy, robust, middle aged business owner, active in church, family, and community, looked forward to retirement a few short years away. Sadly, he suffered a very severe stroke while dressing for work one day. He will never fully recover, and will require specialized care during his remaining life. Result: a family turned upside down.

Case 2: A happily married retired couple. They had planned for retirement wisely, and envisioned travel they had longed for all of their married life. Not long after his retirement, the wife became "different", and was finally diagnosed with dementia. She went downhill fast, and it wasn't long before she had no idea who family was. Result: a family turned upside down.

In both cases, the individuals involved were very spiritually grounded and of strong faith. In neither situation did any family member cave in to "why us" self pity, bitterness, or doubt in their faith. None became angry at God for what had seemed sure to be pleasant retirements gone badly. And, in each case, each family unit stayed as a family unit, fully accepting their new roles as care-givers.

Some cases like these end up badly. There are times when the care-giver simply gives up and bails out, or, worse yet, where the case has ends up as a horrific murder-suicide because there seems to be no other way out. Families have splintered because of situations like these cases.

How we govern our lives, from now until an eventual catastrophic event like this occurs, will govern how we handle such a situation if it happens to us. If God and our faith is at the core of the relationship, and He is the center of our lives, we stand a much better chance of handling such a situation with both dignity and honor. We will continue to love the other, no matter what. We will remain stronger than we otherwise might. And, we will know that no matter what, God hasn't abandoned us.

Bottom Line Thought: While we all hope with all hope that situations like those above will never occur to us, we never know do we? Are you building your foundation in such a manner now that should something like that occur you will be able to deal with it in an honorable and dignified manner? Is your love for your partner strong enough to do that? That's a hard question—or isn't it?

Day 132:
Oxygen

I was walking with a friend once on a day that was overcast, sprinkling slightly, a bit chilly, and it was just gloomy. I happened to mention to him what a crappy day it was. He got quite animated and corrected me. He said, "No! It's a beautiful day out. The sun is out, we just can't see it." I stood corrected about my negative outlook, thanks to his positive one. He was looking at the big picture, I the small.

We've all experienced times like that. We've had days when nothing seemed to go right despite our best intentions and efforts. We've had times when we are strong in our walk, yet the curveballs of life and those little surprises we don't want or expect come at us as if we were being tested. Those are the times we may find ourselves doubting God, or we question Him.

How do we deal with those times? How do we pull it all back together? It isn't always easy to do so is it? Sometimes we simply have to get root level basic and think,

God is like oxygen. We can't see Him, but we can't live without Him.

Bottom Line Thought: That's something that can help us during certain times in our lives, just as it can be used when sharing your faith with a non-believer, isn't it?

Day 133:
Give Up And Give

Give up doubting yourself

Give up negative thinking

Give up fear of failure

Give up criticizing yourself and others

Give up negative self talk

Give up procrastination

Give up fear of success

Give up people pleasing

Give God the chance to work in you and trust that He will

AND

Give thanks to God for loving you so much.

Day 134:
Fairy Tales

When we were small, our parents used to read fairy tales to us before we went to bed. Perhaps that still happens in families. While most of us picture fairy tales as all about glamour, pretty pictures, and happy endings, that really isn't quite so if they are carefully dissected. Some cases in point are:

1. *Cinderella:* Cinderella is held prisoner in her own home where she is treated like a slave. She is subjected to both physical and psychological torment at the hands of her stepmother and stepsisters after the death of her father. That's real happy times isn't it?
2. *Hansel & Greta:* They are abducted by a sadistic maniac who keeps them in captivity in the woods. His plan is to fatten them up and then roast them alive to cannibalize them. That's a real class story for the little guys isn't it?
3. *Little Red Riding Hood:* This girl goes to the forest to visit her grandmother. What does she find there? That granny has been savaged and eaten alive by a wild animal. A darling little story for the kids, right?

Despite the behavioral implications of those fairy tales, they are still being read to children. In no way am I implying that these fairy tales are the driving pin for future behavior of kids. What I am saying is that since they are not true and are just fairy tales full of fantasy why not share stories with our kids that are truth with no fantasy involved?

When have we ever heard of the Bible being called a book of fairy tales? In its entire history it has been challenged and tested, but it remains solid and has never been debunked as untrue. What it has been is a matter of choice for all people. We have the choice to believe the Word, or we can disbelieve it. The stories, parables, and lessons within it all deal with the lives we live in one way or the other, and we can apply it to our lives.

Bottom Line Thought: Whether a father, eventually a father, a grandfather, or just a man of faith, wouldn't you prefer to share life lessons with the children in your life instead of fairy tales based on bad behaviors?

Day 135:
The Butler Did It

In the old movies, the "whodunits", it was not uncommon to hear the lead detective declare "the butler did it", was it? The Sherlock Holmes movies were good for that. Well, they all had to have a story line didn't they?

What are butlers? There are still butlers in today's world. They are dressed up servants with a fancy name. They are a special kind of servant.. Their purpose is to serve at the will of their master, attending to his needs and wants. A butler makes life for his master comfortable. A good butler always does it with class, is humble, and stays in the background and is faithful and loyal. Their job is a lifetime job of selfless servitude.

It's not a real stretch to say we are all butlers is it, if we so choose? We are all called to serve at the will of our master—God. We are asked to serve faithfully and loyally, be humble, and make it a lifetime choice. The only difference in being a servant for God is that we serve Him by serving others. In that sense, there are pastors, church staff members, and other ministry partners, many of whom are full time servants.

But what about us—the ordinary folk who are butlers called to serve? We don't need any education, special talents, background, or particular abilities to serve. We are special because we have willing hearts. We can serve in such ways as;

- A volunteer for one of the teams at church—the traffic team, the set-up team, the cleaning team, office team, maintenance team, grounds team, or any of the other project teams the church may have.
- As a story teller or helper for the kids ministry. Most kid's ministries need male role models to be a part of their team.
- Find and "adopt" an elderly couple or a widow or widower. Many will need such simple things as transportation, mowing, a meal once in a while, etc.
- As a family, take food to the local homeless encampment. They are out there.

Bottom Line Thought: The butler did it. Is there any reason that can't be said of you? What's to stop you from being one of God's servants in different ways?

Day 136:
You Never Know

I attended a men's breakfast a few years back, and I was fascinated by the conversation of one of the men there. Lyle was a successful businessman with whom I had done business. He opened his remarks by saying, "I can't wait to get to Heaven." That got the attention of those of us sitting around him at the table.

Lyle then went on to explain why he said that. His words are paraphrased due to the time that has passed since I heard them (a nice way of saying my memory isn't what it used to be). He said;

"All of our lives we come in contact with others. We often know very little about the people. I just can't begin to imagine how exciting it will be to get to Heaven and have a perfect stranger come up to me and say 'Thank you.' Since I wouldn't what he was talking about he would go on to explain—'years ago, Lyle, you didn't know what I was going through, but we were talking and you said just the right thing. It was what you said that got me to think about my relationship with God. You planted a seed in me which eventually grew, and it grew to the point where I am here today, a place where I have the chance to meet you again and say thank you.'"

Lyle then stressed that it is all of the little things we can do that could be a pivotal moment, or the tipping point, in another person's life. He suggested that we may never know whether something we say or do may trigger a spiritual awakening in someone we run across. He concluded his remarks with "you just never know."

His comments made me think about my own awakening. There were no bells or whistles, no pleas, no pressure. There were just some passing comments that planted that very first seed.

Bottom Line Thought: It seemed as if Lyle had made it his mission to be comfortable, real, and openly honest with the folks he came in contact with, as well as wearing his faith on his sleeve. You are not Lyle, but you have the same opportunities as he had. Are you open to them? Wouldn't it be nice to have that stranger walk up and say thanks some day? You never know.

Day 137:
A Blood Bath

Sometimes we feel grungy don't we? Maybe we aren't really dirty—we just feel like it. What do we do? We take a bath or shower, both of which most consider a feel good thing. After a nice shower or bath we feel clean, content, and happy to feel clean.

Doing life sometimes makes us feel grungy as well. Because of our brokenness, some of the things we do out of habit, the sin in our lives, or just the stuff we have to deal with makes us feel unclean inside doesn't it? None of us are immune to that. It's heart dirt that is making us feel unclean, a grunginess of our soul. Jumping into the shower or bath isn't going to change that one bit.

The only means of cleaning heart dirt or soul grunge is a blood bath. It's the best bath available for that type of cleansing. It doesn't take any water and we don't have to dry off (except possibly our tears), and we don't have to change clothes.

A blood bath is when we take the time to stop, reflect on our present conditions, and focus on the magnitude of what Christ did us. He died for us. It was His blood that washed away our sins, and still does. It's a blood bath we commemorate when we take communion. But we don't have to wait until communion to take our bath. We can do that at any time that our grungy soul and dirty heart requires a bath.

Bottom Line Thought: Think of it this way—the blood baths you take are the best baths you will ever take. They will renew you like none other.

Day 138:
Figure It Out

A boss will sometimes be approached by an employee who has a question about a project, and will simply states "figure it out." We do that sometimes with our kids as well—"you figure it out" Or, there is a family problem and we may say to our wife, "Well, figure it out." In those cases there are several ways they can interpret our response;

- "I'm too busy and I don't want to be bothered right now."
- Or, it can be an implied encouragement to do something on our own.

Either way, it becomes a guessing exercise for us. What did the person who said it mean? Doesn't he care? We can have conflicting thoughts about it.

What do we do when we have some serious life questions we are trying to find answers to? They may be questions like;

- My spiritual life is in trouble. What do I do?
- I have questions about my relationship with God. How do I handle that?
- I have relational issues and I don't know what to do.
- I can't seem to stop doing things I know are wrong.

How would we like to hear "you figure it out" when we have those kind of issues facing us? There is one single source of complete help, information, inspiration, and truth available to us. It's called the Bible. The Bible never once says "you figure it out." What it does say over and over is "trust God." That's because He's already got it all figured out. So in the times we need an answer we can go to the book, we can pray, or we can seek the counsel of a godly person we are close to. We'll never get a "you figure it out."

Bottom Line Thought: Do you abdicate your responsibility as a man and father by saying "you figure it out" when it isn't necessary? Do you know where to go when you can't figure it out?

Day 139:
School Of Hard Knocks

Even though I finished college and then completed my Masters Degree at middle age, when someone asks about my education I always answer that I got a PhD from the School of Hard Knocks—with honors. Many of us went there didn't we?

It was my attendance there that prompted me to pen the lyrics for a country song I wrote—*All I Ever Did Right, was Everything Wrong*. It takes attendance at that fine institution to wake some of us up doesn't it? Some of the courses I particularly focused on while attending were;

- Stupid Choices and Decision Making 101. I aced that one.
- Yielding to Temptation 302. I had a hard time quitting that course.
- Maintaining Loss of Self Control 405. One of my favorites.
- Sabotaging Good Relationships 202. I got an A++ in that one.
- Ego Building 104. A perennial offering I really enjoyed.
- Why You Don't Need God 206. The curriculum was wild!

Hard Knocks University turns out some of the finest broken people in the world. One of its shortcomings is that they don't teach how to handle the baggage that comes with the course work.

Luckily for all of us, a degree from that place doesn't have to be a permanent mark on our record. We can get a better degree from Christian University. It's a worldwide school, housed in churches, with satellite facilities known as small or community groups. We can even attend this University in our own homes. If we choose to attend, we will find;

Jesus is the Principal

The Holy Spirit is our teacher

Other Christians are our classmates

The Bible is the study book

Trials, errors, and temptation are our exams

Winning others for Christ is our assignment

Prayer is our attendance

Grace and redemption are the lockers for our baggage

The Crown of Life is our degree

Praise and worship is the motto

And, Heaven is the graduation present.

I'm glad I decided to attend CU. What a difference it has made in my life. What a difference it makes in all of our lives.

Bottom Line Thought: Have you decided to be alumni yet? At which school?

Day 140:
The Marriage Box

> The Marriage Box
>
> Most people get married believing a myth that marriage is a beautiful box full of all the things they have longed for; companionship, intimacy, friendship, etc. The truth is that marriage at the start is an empty box. You must put something in it before you can take anything out. There is no love in marriage. Love is in people. And people put love in marriage. There is no romance in marriage. You have to infuse it into your marriage. A couple must learn the art and form, the habit of giving, loving, serving, praising, keeping the box full. If you take out more than you put in, the box will be empty.

Unknown source

Bottom Line Thought: Though we and the box may get old, we are still us, and the box is still the box. Young or old, the only thing that changes is how much we put into, or take out of, the box. Are you doing all you can to keep your box full?

Day 141:
Men And Boys

"The difference between men and boys is the size of their toys"

That statement's been around for a while. It's a statement of one-upmanship, of ego, and misused privilege mostly used by the men with the fanciest and fastest cars, the larger sleeker boats, etc. It can be seen in action by taking a quick trip down to Burnham Harbor on Chicago's lakefront. There one will see some very large and fancy yachts, amongst the smaller fishing boats. This is not a reflection of all who are fortunate enough to have the "toys", per se. It does, however, address the attitude that often comes by owning such.

When it comes to real life matters, where the stakes are high, where the prize is eternity in Heaven, where we have to know Christ in order to reach that prize, there is a huge difference between the men and the boys.

> Here's to all the real men out there. Boys play house, men build homes. Boys shack up, men get married. Boys make babies, men raise children. A boy won't raise his own children. A man will raise someone else's. Boys invent excuses for failure. Men produce strategies for success. Boys look for someone to take care of them. Men look for someone to take care of. Boys seek popularity. Men demand respect, and know how to give it.

The real difference between the men and the boys isn't their toys. It's whether they are Christ centered or not. A real man can own that 35 foot fancy yacht just as a boy can.

Bottom Line Thought: Regardless what toys you have, have you grown up to be a real man yet?

Day 142:
A Matter Of Perspective

My mom used to call me a "happy little optimist." I took after her. She always seemed "up" despite constant and pressing medical issues most of her life, and the ensuing financial drain on the family budget. We were poor, and she was "up." I learned from those issues and her attitude, and grew up into one whose cup was always half full instead of half empty. Her issues also taught me to see the good in people instead of looking for the bad.

GOOD

What do we read in that graphic? Many will read evil, but some will see good the first time they look. It's the same in our lives. Many will immediately see suspected evil in people and situations, and their focus will remain there, affording them little opportunity to see any good that may be present. Others will see the good in them, and that will allow them to build upon that good and help grow that person or improve the situation. There will be times when all that anyone, regardless of perspective, sees is absolutely nothing but pure unadulterated evil. That is a different situation altogether.

We all know that there is good and evil in this world. Seeing evil (shall we say sin) in our first encounter with average, everyday people and situations is like looking into a tunnel and saying "it's dark in here." By seeing those same people and situations as good, we are looking into that same tunnel, but adding "but there is light at the end of that tunnel."

When we see the good first, and recognize that there may be evil (sin) there, we have the opportunity to let our light be *the* light in that tunnel if we are truly men of God.

Bottom Line Thought: Could looking for the good first change your perspective of people and situations, and thus let you use your light to light the way for them to change their lives?

Day 143:
The Beast Within: Anger

We have some beasts living within us. In some of us, the beast(s) may be active, or they may be dormant—but they're there. I had a friend who shared this with me long before he passed on: "We are born with sin. We learn to deal with it, but it's still there. It's like a snake lying curled up in the sun. It lays there still so you might think it was dead. But every once in a while it'll poke its head up, look around, and if everything is ok, it will go back to sleep. But sometimes it stays up just to stir things up."

We have a beast in us called anger. It's like that snake. It will poke its head up to remind us that we still have it, and sometimes it will stir things up to prove that point. Anger, in and of itself is good for us, and especially when it's not over-the-top self righteous anger. As the opposite of happiness, we need anger in our lives, but it has to be controlled and appropriately used.

The problem some have with anger is that it has become a predictably unpredictable side of us. Those around us don't know if we are going to just get angry, or if we are going to ingloriously explode in anger. It is our uncontrolled anger that gets us in trouble, and it harms our relationships. It helps destroy trust, and it can ruin transparency in those around us, simply because they "clam up" because they don't know when or if the next explosion will come, nor how bad it will be.

An anger that isn't controlled causes us to say things we never should and do things we shouldn't do. When we are experiencing it, it will drive us because we have traded in our ability for rational thought for it. It has become the snake once lying in the sun. It has become provoked and it will strike in a very ugly way, leaving unwanted damage and injury behind. It is not godly, nor are our actions at that point.

Bottom Line Thought: Remember the serpent in the Garden of Eden? It is representative of the beast within us, of which anger is one. Do you allow anger to take over at inappropriate times and in an unwanted manner?

Day 144:
The Beast Within: Greed

One of the beasts within us, greed, is one that stands in the way of our developing a solid and lasting relationship with Christ. When we become so fixated on our "stuff" and need for more, we begin to lose focus of what true satisfaction is. Instead, our focus turns to our wants instead of our needs, and we become driven or obsessed on what we have to have.

Some will think that greed just affects those who have wealth or are well off. Greed is one of those snakes within us that we all have to one degree or another, rich or poor. It's normal to want things, and especially when we need them. But it's not okay to want them if they are the driving force of our lives. Many families have proven that as they now live check to check, or in debt, because of greed.

Greed is the inward force that causes us to think that all we have is ours, instead of all we have we owe. Our focus should be on this; all that we have we owe to God, because it is by His blessing and His grace that we have it. In that vein, we are thus spiritually obliged to give a portion back for Kingdom work in this world we live in. Our greed can prevent us from doing that.

Greed can harm our relationships when it becomes our focus. Our "stuff" and money becomes more important than people and God. It becomes a sin when it replaces either of those. Thus, wealth and financial stability and comfort can be either a blessing or a curse. It's a blessing when it is of, for, and by God in the mind of the one so benefitted, or it is a curse if it is viewed only as a personal accomplishment. Above all, greed is an equal opportunity sin—anyone can be bitten by that snake.

Bottom Line Thought: Do you suffer from the disease of Monster of More? Does it affect your relationship with others and with God? Does it drive you, and what you do? Do you share what you have for Kingdom work?

Day 145:
The Beast Within: Laziness

Laziness is one of the 7 beasts living within us. It is scripturally referred to as sloth. When we think of laziness we think of one who just lies around doing nothing, or at best, just being minimally active. We'll think of laziness when we say something like "he's too lazy to go get a job", or "he's too lazy to do what needs to be done around the house." Those *may* be examples of laziness, but perhaps not always so. He may just have a medical condition that prevents him from working and we are unaware of it, etc.

The beast called laziness is not selective at all. It resides in all of us to one degree or another. For example;

- Do we have spiritual apathy?
  - Is continually growing as a Christian man a priority in our lives?
  - Has being the spiritual leader of our family been abdicated to someone else or been completely dropped as a role?
- Do we have emotional apathy?
  - Do we care more for ourselves than others?
  - Are our hearts hardened to any show of emotions or openess?

Laziness in the above context also means that we will refuse to meet, or be careless in our obligations—especially our spiritual, moral, and legal ones. It also can corrupt our willingness to waste or not recognize our talents and gifts to further the Kingdom work. It will stunt our excitement about the role Jesus has in our lives and we can become complacent and inactive in our active spiritual activities. When that happens, we are opening the door for sin to come into our lives and fill the void.

Bottom Line Thought: Okay, maybe you might sleep in once in a while and miss church. But let's think about real laziness—like the ones that will really affect you as a Christ follower and your relationships. Are you the spiritual leader of your family? Do you care more about yourself than others? Does your apathy affect your obligations as a man? Is there sin in your life because of your laziness to do something about it?

Day 146:
The Beast Within: Pride

Of the beasts within all of us, pride is perhaps the most interesting because there are 2 kinds of pride. There is good and welcomed pride (virtuous), and there is the pride that is destructive and cancerous to us (vice). Let's take a look at them by breaking down some of the opposing characteristics of each one.

- Pride is a virtue when we have a sense of self-satisfaction with our choices and decision (humility is shown here). It becomes a vice when we have an over-inflated sense of satisfaction over those same choices and actions and need to point that out to everyone around us (ego is on display here).
- It's a virtue when we are satisfied with ourselves, our lot in life, and we are comfortable in our own skin. It is a vice when we feel the need to engage in one-upmanship with those around us.
- It is a virtue when we quietly appreciate what we have and do in life (honest and thankful appreciation). It is a vice when we need to know that everyone else around us knows what we have and do in life (hubris or chutzpah).
- Pride is a virtue when we are proud of our families, as individuals and as a group collectively. It becomes a vice when the bragging begins.
- It is a virtue when we are proud of our spiritual growth and our ability as we quietly use our talents and gifts to help others. It is a vice when we are pious about our spiritual selves and feel the need to flaunt our Christianity.

Pride truly shows the difference between letting our light shine, and showing our light shining as we do this thing called life.

Bottom Line Thought: As men, pride strongly tugs at us at times, sometimes in the most innocuous ways. Do you find ego creeping in your thoughts as opposed to humility? Do you sometimes consider yourself better than others? Are you quietly comfortable with yourself and your status, or do you get the urge to share it inappropriately to others around you? Do you quietly go about the business of your spiritual growth?

Day 147:
The Beast Within: Lust

This beast within us is almost universally the one we are most secretive about and the one that most powerfully affects us. Lust is, simply, an emotion or feeling of intense desire in the body. It's a psychological force that creates a very strong, often intense, wanting or desire for an object or a circumstance which will fulfill the emotion. Grossly overweight folks may have a lust for food. It could probably be safe to assume that Imelda Marcos, the former First Lady of the Philippines lusted for shoes. She had over 3,000 pairs. Neither of those are secretive lusts—the evidence of those lusts are apparent.

Sexual lust is the leading secretive lust. It's the lust that plagues many men. Volumes have been written about it and tons of psychological studies have addressed it. Many offenders are incarcerated because of it, and many marriages have been destroyed by it. Here are some basics about it:

- Many men can't look at a beautiful woman and look at her as just a woman gifted with good looks. They look at her comparatively with questions about how it would be to be with her, often in a sexual, or at least a fantasizing manner.
- Oftentimes, a man's lust will lead him to pornography of varied kinds.
    - Idle times will often drive that lust, sometimes inappropriately.
- Sometimes a man's lust will lead him to extramarital affairs, or worse.
- At times a man can't keep his eyes off of a nice looking waitress, a group of girls hanging out together, or the like, even when with his family or friends. Even though he may try his hardest not to, he has a difficult time not taking "sneak peeks."
- Lust is not easily defeated, and tends to do exactly what ego's do to us by easing God out of our thinking and our hearts.

Lust, is, I believe, the one beast within that is the most easily recognized as wrong by the men who struggle with it. Therefore they are very secretive about it. They know their thoughts are not within society's norm. The destruction to men and their relationships is also the most visible to others. The fight against lust is best done with a strong partner—God.

Bottom Line Thought: A strong enemy puts up a good fight. If you lust, how do you battle it?

Day 148:
The Beast Within: Envy

Envy, unlike lust for instance, is an emotion that affects us. We become envious when we look at others and try to compare ourselves to them. If we see, and envision, achievement, possessions, quality of life, wealth, status, and the like in others and either wish we had what they had, or wish they didn't, we are envious. Envy encourages unhappiness in the one experiencing it, but it can also, in cases, lead to subtle sabotage of the others efforts at continued good fortune. That pretty much expresses what we could call destructive or harmful (to us or others) envy. There is a good form of envy as well, for example; the downtrodden segment of society can rightfully be envious of those not as poorly off as they. That is benign envy, and it can bring about social change.

Envy, to us ordinary men can cause us to do some uncharacteristic, and sometimes habit forming things. It can feed our desire, because of the unhappiness caused by it, to feel the need to "keep up with the Joneses." For example, if the neighbors keep an extraordinarily beautiful yard we might allow that mild envy to spend more than we have available to upgrade our own, perhaps at the expense of buying the family a much needed new couch. Or, if one of the guys recently bought a new boat, it could cause us to think we should have one (and perhaps actually buy one), even though doing so might cause a family budget crunch or prevent money from going into the college fund for the kids.

Envy may be one of the easier beasts within to conquer, simply from the fact that many time our sense of reality and necessity will prevail at times when tempted. That said, there may be instances when our envy can stand in the way of our happiness and well being. If we were to envy another man's wife in such a way that it turned to flirtations and lust, a relational envy, serious consequences could be a result relationally.

Bottom Line Thought: If you are fully secure in all that you are, all that you do, and who you are, you will be a happy and contented person. If not, you may have an issue with envy. Do you know if you have an envy issue or not?

Day 149:
The Beast Within: Gluttony

We, with little doubt, have *all* experienced a bout or two of gluttony. It happens to me every time I go to my favorite buffet! For those of you who may have doubts about yourself, just think family picnics, Thanksgiving with a full house (and table), or even the card game with the boys that goes on late into the night. Think unlimited beer and snacks.

Those are all indications of gluttony. Are those examples a bad form of gluttony? Of course they aren't. Eating like a starving dog or eating like a pig once in a while hardly qualifies as gluttony. If that's the case, then what is gluttony? Let's look at that.

- One might consider a person who amasses vast wealth and lives strictly for that purpose, with no intent of ever using any of that wealth to help others less fortunate, to be a glutton.
- Or, perhaps a person lives in such extravagance with so much waste. That is gluttony.
- On a more blue collar level, one whose needs are amply met that won't make any effort to help the needy may be a glutton.
- On a different level, if one is excited about his Christianity and has been successful in changing his life because of it, might not he be a glutton by not sharing what God has done for and with him with anyone who may be seeking?

Gluttony is an issue any time we have enough and don't even consider sharing with others. We don't have to be wealthy to be gluttonous. Gluttony isn't restricted to just food and drink and money. No matter what our position in life is, we all have abilities, talents, and gifts we can share to help make the lives of others better. If we are stingy with those things, no matter our reason, we are gluttonous.

Bottom Line Thought: Does this help you consider a new outlook of gluttony? It's not just about food and wealth. It's about all we have and are and whether we have the heart to share with others or not.

Day 150:
Death

I found an old worn clipping that addressed the topic of death. There was no indication on the clipping about where it came from, from whom, or when it was originally written. It addressed death in a spiritual way.

> Death
>
> A very sick man turned to his doctor as he was preparing to leave the examining room and said, "Doctor, I am afraid to die. Tell me what lies on the other side."
>
> Very quietly, the doctor said, "I don't know..."
>
> "You don't know? You're a Christian man and yet you don't know what's on the other side?" the sick man asked.
>
> The doctor was holding the handle of another door to the office; on the other side came the sound of scratching and whining, and as he opened the door, a dog sprang into the room and leaped on him with an eager show of gladness. Turning to the patient, the doctor asked, "Did you notice my dog? He's never been in this room before. He didn't know what was inside. He knew nothing except that his master was here, and when the door opened, he sprang in without fear. I know little of what is on the other side of death, but I do know 1 thing—I know my Master is there and that is enough."

Younger folks often have a sense of invincibility about themselves. They don't think about death. As they get older that changes, but just a little. In their middle age years they begin to think about it more often, and by the time retirement age comes around they realize that we aren't invincible, that we will die. One of the surest ways to come to the attitude of the good doctor in the above story is to live every day with the personal motto—*"I want to know Christ."*

No matter what our stage of life or spiritual growth, if we will try faithfully to live by that motto, we will never have any questions about what is on the other side when we die. It will be an unknown, but we know it will be a unknown. We will have the faith to not fear death, and the strength to face it head on.

Bottom Line Thought: You will die. We all do. Can you look at it with strong faith?

Day 151:
Things He Doesn't See

In my early youth we always dutifully dressed up on Sunday mornings and went to Sunday School which was followed by church. Here's what I remember about it;

- In Sunday School they talked about this guy who we couldn't see, who sees everything we do. We could see pretty pictures of His Son, Jesus, but there never were any pictures of God.
- The talk about God seeing everything we do and hearing everything we say was pretty scary to me. It felt oppressive, like I was being spied on all the time.
- We always heard about Jesus loving us, but never heard that the one who spied on us loved us.
- Knowing now what I didn't know then makes that past seem pretty messed up.

I'm not sure how much of that past experience affected me as I grew up into a man who managed to stay on the darker side of life for a very long time. I do know that one of the thoughts in my mind was that if this God saw and heard everything I did I was already doomed. Why should I bother to change.

Obviously, things have changed drastically in my thinking by now. From all I have learned since accepting Christ, I now know that there are 3 things God doesn't see;

1. He doesn't see any person who has not sinned.
2. He doesn't see any sinner He doesn't love.
3. He doesn't see any sinner He cannot save.

Because of those three things, we can know that He's not just an ogre "up there, somewhere", but rather a God that knows us and unconditionally loves us. We have an awesome God, we do. He is an equal opportunity lover and saver of sinners and that's a very good thing for people like me. Is there a 'Yea God" in the house?

Bottom Line Thought; Could you use the truths of the 3 things God doesn't see in your toolbox for helping bring others to Christ and help dispel some of their erroneous thinking about Gods role if they have any?

Day 152:
When The Planes Stopped Flying

The date, 9-11-2001 is imprinted in the minds of most people today. It was a day of enormous tragedy, shock, and horror for all Americans as we watched the Twin Towers in New York City brought down by a couple of airliners hijacked by some terrorists.

Because of the unknowns following the attack, the FAA ordered all airliners within the continental limits of the United States to be grounded immediately, no matter where they were. In a short time there were no planes flying in the sky. The skies became quiet. Street traffic was at a minimum because people were staying put to take in the on-going news of the shocking attack. It was eerily quiet most of the day, and a lot of personal introspection took place I imagine. Prayerfully, we as a nation will never, ever, have to experience anything like that day again.

In our lives as men doing a constant juggling act of being men, fathers, husbands, providers, spiritual leaders, employees, and more, there are times when the planes in our head need to stop flying. We need quiet for our minds and soul. We need _quality_ quiet, not for just a few moments, but for enough time for us to clearly hear and feel God. We know (hopefully) of God's presence in our lives, but when was the last time we deliberately took the time to *just be quiet* to hear what He might be trying to say to us?

The ultimate example of the need for individual quiet for the purpose of listening to what God wants to tell us was set by Jesus. Throughout His ministry, at multiple times He simply went off alone to a quiet place to hear His Father.

Bottom Line Thought: Have you tried having a truly individual quiet time with God? What do you suppose you might hear from Him? Can you give Him some time, with no distractions, just you and Him? Can you ground the airplanes in your head for just a half hour each day for that purpose?

HINT: If you get that far and you find that stuff starts wandering in your mind, simply sit with a hand facing upward on each knee. When the stuff starts in the mind, simply turn the hand over and symbolically "dump the stuff."

Day 153:
Truck Drivers

The professional drivers of the 18 wheelers, those large semi tractor trailers that are such a vital part of our economy because they move so many goods, are considered to be among the safest drivers. They respect the fact that they are carrying large loads in big trucks that can do a lot of damage to other vehicles if they were to drive them recklessly. Overall, they are also considered the more considerate of drivers.

In many ways, it wouldn't be a bad idea if we chose to conduct our lives like those truckers drive would it? There are some subtle lessons we could learn;

- To pace ourselves and plan ahead for the trip of life.
- To live at a steady pace, fast enough to get there but slow enough to really enjoy the ride.
- To be economically wise so as to have plenty for our trip.
- To be cautious and aware of our surroundings so we would be prepared for any emergency.
- To be patient and tolerant with others who might otherwise drive us crazy.
- To fully know our own limits.
- To only carry a load we can handle.
- To be courteous to all around us.
- To share our road with others.
- To take the time to pull over and stop to help someone in need.
- To get to our destination safely.

Sometimes we are too wrapped up in our own little world to be the Christian men we really can be. Maybe we need to think like those professional truck drivers.

Bottom Line Thought: Can you give a big 10-4 to those ideas? Could they apply to you in your daily drive of life?

Day 154:
A Child's Prayer

One of the most beautiful things I like to see is a group of little kids singing "Jesus Loves Me." They are so serious and enthusiastic, and they sing it like they really mean it, especially when they get to the end--"because the Bible tells me so." They seem to put emphasis on that part, like they know it, and they are so proud. It sounds like an expression of blind faith. When it is an especially moving song is when our children kneel down for prayer at bedtime and sing that song.

Whenever I hear that it brings to mind the times when I was a kid in Sunday School, when life was so much simpler. In thinking of those days I feel that life was overall much more pure, less complex, and in general the mores and values were at such a higher level than in today's times. Perhaps many of us think of how things were then as compared to present times, and long for them.

We actually have far more control over our own lives then we may realize. We can, if we choose to, simplify our lives and make them less complex. We can instill in our families the values and mores we once had and now cherish as memories. We can go back in time when we sang that song and sense how we felt as we sang it. And, in doing so, we will open ourselves to a new level of child-like innocence, if even for just a moment, a moment that will feel delightfully clean, innocent, and simple.

Maybe, if we took the time to fully enjoy the moment, it would move us to seek more of those moments in little ways in our lives. And, maybe, if we did that we would be more open to what God has to say to us about a simpler way of life, one that would be more God honoring. I have to wonder how we, as adults, would feel about singing that children's song as a prayer during worship time at church.

Bottom Line Thought: Can you kill a couple of birds with one stone by singing that song with your kids as they prepare for bedtime?

Day 155:
A Little Extra Light

There are certain times in our lives when events or circumstances dictate that we need a little extra light to get things back to normal;

- When the house lights go out at night because a circuit breaker popped.
- When we're on a trip and encounter a long tunnel.
- When we're out walking our dog at night and the street lights are out.
- When our lives are in a mess and all we see is darkness.

In most circumstances when all we see is darkness, we can rectify that simply by using a flashlight. It's a different issue altogether when all we see in our lives is darkness because of what we are facing or have to deal with. Rayovac™ doesn't make flashlights for that.

FAITH is seeing light with your heart,
When all your eyes see is darkness.

Faith is ours to choose to use when Rayovac™ won't do the job. Faith is part of God's home within us. It is always well lit, and its rays are hope, calm, security, joy, and peace and most of all it is a *darkness busting love for us*. We all have the ability, and the choice, to look away from the darkness, and look toward the light of God's love, and all that it brings to us. That's not a little extra light. It's a whole lot of light when we need it most.

Bottom Line Thought: Did you know you have to change batteries in your flashlight to keep a steady source of light, and that you never have to change the batteries in God's light. Faith never fails.

Day 156:
The Starfish Story

A fellow by the name of Loren Eiseley (1907—1977) penned many bits of inspiration during his time. One was The Starfish Story which has apparently taken on many forms by others over the years. I was sent a meme of the story a while back and was struck by its message which I am sharing here.

Once upon a time, there was a wise man who used to go to the ocean to do his writing. He had a habit of walking on the beach before he began his work. One day, as he was walking along the shore, he looked down the beach and saw a human figure moving like a dancer. He smiled to himself at the thought of someone who would dance to the day, so he walked faster to catch up.

As he got closer, he noticed that the figure was that of a young man, and that what he was doing was not dancing at all. The young man was reaching down to the shore and picking up small objects, and throwing them into the ocean. He came closer still and called out, "Good morning! May I ask what is it that you are doing?"

They young man paused, looked up, and replied, "Throwing starfish into the ocean."

"I must ask, then, why are you throwing starfish into the ocean?" asked the somewhat startled wise man.

To this, the young man replied, "The sun is up and the tide is going out. If I don't throw them in, they will die."

Upon hearing this, the wise man commented, "But, young man, do you not realize that there are miles and miles of beach and there are starfish all along every mile. You can't possibly make a difference!"

At this, the young man bent down, picked up yet another starfish, and threw it into the ocean. As it met the water, he said, "It made a difference for that one."

The starfish on the beach are not all that much different than us humans here on earth. Someone, the young man, took the time to help the ones he could get back into better circumstances. He knew he couldn't save them all, but he didn't shy away from making a difference in the lives of those he could.

Bottom Line Thought: You too can make a difference in the lives of others.

Day 157:
We Don't Know

Birth..........................Death

We know with certainty that we were born, and that we will die. What we don't know, nor will we ever, are how many dots there will be between the two.

Are you making every dot count? Are you honoring God with each dot? Are you thanking God for each dot? In the short span between birth and death, every dot counts. After death the dots are endless in Heaven. That's all the reason we need to be concerned how we live our dots while here on earth.

Day 158:
Why A Christian?

Some folks may wonder why they are Christians in their moments of reflection. Some may think that it's needed given their background. There are some who have been brought up as Christians and have remained so, and haven't tasted the fruit of the tree. Others may have a need to have something in their lives besides themselves. Others are spiritually convicted to be Christians.

Whatever our reasons, or whenever we made the decision to be Christians and live the Christian life, we probably experienced an "ah-ha" moment in our lives. We made the choice because it was the only logical and reasonable choice for us to make at the time and we started to experience some change within us in a relatively short time. That change was sometimes scary and surreal, it could have been very obvious or somewhat obscure, but it was there. It was a real change.

I found a little saying that sums it up for my experience;

I'm not a Christian because I'm strong and have it all together.

I'm a Christian because I'm weak and admit that I need a savior.

That's enough to give anyone an "ah-ha" moment. When it happened to me I'm pretty sure it gave God one too as He surely must have said, "It finally happened. I waited a long time for this."

Real men will never question why they are Christians. They will know why. It's because real men acknowledge their weaknesses and admit their need for a savior in their lives. So the better question to ask becomes, "Why not be a Christian?"

Bottom Line Thought: Why are you a Christian?

Day 159:
In A Rut

A few years ago we took a road trip to see the Skywalk over the Grand Canyon. When we got near there on a 2 lane paved road, we found we had to turn off of the nice road and travel on 20+ miles on a narrow gravel road that was a very twisty, hilly, rutty, dusty, and windy road to get there. There were signs posted, warning of the need to use caution because of the conditions. The scenery on that "road" was beautiful, but enjoying it was limited because of the need to pay attention to the conditions of the road and other traffic.

In our everyday *and* spiritual lives we sometimes find ourselves in a rut don't we? There is a difference between being in a rut, and having to drive through ruts to see the Grand Canyon. In the former, we let it happen to us. In the latter we choose the ruts.

How do we come to feel as if we are in a rut in our daily and/or spiritual lives? We choose not to find joy in what we are doing, no matter what it is. We allow ourselves to be okay with the sameness of our lives, and that apathy changes to boredom. We fail to find those things that add excitement and energy to our lives, and we become stale inside. We are in a rut. We often fail to see all that is good around us as a result because we feel smothered by the walls of the rut. It also happens with our love for those we are in relationship with.

Being in a rut can bring damage to each aspect of our lives as we begin to feel unworthy or useless because of it. We often feel helpless. Our zest for life suffers because of the slow progression of the feeling. It's not something that envelopes us all of a sudden. Being in a rut is like a cancer that slowly grows within us.

This is somewhat of a negative read isn't it? It is meant to be that way, because on the next page we'll read about how to get out of the rut.

Bottom Line Thought: Do you sometimes think that your life, spiritual walk, and/or your relationship is in a rut? Are you losing sight of the beauty and benefit of each?

Day 160:
Out Of The Rut

As humans we may feel as if we are in a rut at times. Some will feel that way more often than others. Either way, there are things that we can do to get rid of that negative feeling we have about ourselves.

1. Don't hide from the fact that we feel that way. Recognize it, own it, and understand that it doesn't make you a "bad" you. It's a normal phase that can happen to any of us.
2. Superman can stop bullets. He can't stop himself from feeling like he is in a rut at times.
3. .If you feel you're in a relational rut, talk about it with your partner. Talk about how to turn it into a positive. Maybe you need date nights or spontaneous fun times together—anything to attack the sameness of the relationship. Two attacking a problem is much more effective at making change than one.
4. If it is a spiritual rut, talk about it and pray about it. Perhaps there is stuff that is going on in your spiritual life that you need to be transparent about and you aren't. Maybe you have started to question yourself as a Christian man. Transparency and communication are the keys to answering those questions.
5. Being in a rut is not an event. It is a process that has led you there. Once you have accepted that, come up with a rut-busting plan. Implement it, follow it, and enjoy the ride back to joy, peace, and contentment.
6. See forward. Keep your focus in front of you, not behind you, and savor every positive sign of change. That, in and of itself, becomes infectious and healing.
7. Don't be down on yourself for what is a natural, temporary feeling. Love yourself for seeing it and doing something about it. Trust that God will be there to walk with you as you go through it. And know that you are honoring Him with this effort.

Rut-itis is just a temporary thing. It becomes a permanent issue only if we choose it to be. Most of us, however, don't enjoy ourselves when we make that wrong choice.

Bottom Line Thought: The roller coaster of normal life gives us peaks and valleys—and ruts. None of them last. Is any part of your life in a rut? How do you deal with the ruts in your life?

Day 161:
12 Simple Things

We are all in relationship of some sort with others, unless we are complete hermits. There is no escaping the fact that we interact with others in our lives. If we all did the following 12 simple things we can do in *all* of our relationships with *all* others, can you imagine what our lives would be like? For that matter, theirs too!

1. Show everyone kindness and respect
2. Give people we don't know a fair chance.
3. Accept others just the way they are.
4. Do little things every day for others.
5. Pay attention to who our real friends are.
6. Stay in touch with people who matter to us.
7. Keep our promises and tell the truth.
8. Say what we mean and mean what we say.
9. Allow other to make their own decisions.
10. Talk a little less, and listen a lot more.
11. Leave petty arguments alone.
12. Ignore unconstructive, hurtful commentary.

Obviously, one could immediately come to the conclusion that those 12 items should apply to the anonymous keyboard warriors on social media. I would agree. But, isn't it far more important that we apply them to ourselves in our everyday face to face relationships? What a world it might be if those 12 items were at the core of our relational skills. How pleasing would that be to the God that loves us? How would they, if we applied them to ourselves, help us in our Christian walk as men?

Bottom Line Thought: If you did a little checklist on yourself with all of the relationships you come in contact with, how would you score from a 1 to 12?

Day 162:
I'm Sorry

I know someone who says that a lot, many times with a tone of voice. The trouble is, they don't really mean it very often, because they are the type of person who is *very* seldom wrong in their own mind. Those kinds of folks are challenges to be around aren't they?

Don't we sometimes kind of whip the old "I'm sorry" out in our own relationships without really meaning it? We use that version of I'm sorry to end the discussion because it might get a bit uncomfortable if it were to go further.

I'm sorry can be either an empty term, or it can be the most sincere heartfelt exclamation we can make. Whichever version we use will determine the value we place on the relationship. There's no in between. We either value the relationship, or we think more of ourselves and winning, than we think of the other.

> Sorry is not enough.
> Sometimes we actually have to change.

Here's the end cap for the subject—the difference between a real I'm sorry and a pretend one is the real one will not only sound real, it will have a "will you forgive me" following it. Capiche?

Bottom Line Thought: If you found this topic doesn't apply to you, I'm sorry, will you please forgive me? My guess would be that won't be the case will it?

Day 163:
Woman

"And God made woman....", or a similar phrase is at the front of most, if not all, versions of the Bible. I was sent an unattributed meme about woman, and found the message interesting—and appropriate for men. It said;

> Woman
>
> was made from the rib of a man.
>
> not from his head to top him,
>
> nor his foot to be stepped on by him,
>
> but from his side to be equal to him,
>
> under his arm to be protected by him,
>
> and near his heart to be loved by him.

Some men have some pretty awful beliefs or thoughts about women don't they? Those thoughts might not be obvious. They may view them as subservient, as sex objects, as second class, as "property", or worse. God made women as equals. He didn't make them so Adam could have a sex object or a servant to serve him.

If we, as Christian men, look at all women in our lives as *anything but* our equals, we have a problem, don't we? How God honoring is that?

Bottom Line Thought: Does your worldview of women line up with your spiritual view of women?

Day 164:
Whining

You read it right. It is whining with an "h" in it, not winning. Why whining in a book for men? Certainly men don't whine—or do they? Let's put it this way—winning starts when the whining stops. Here are a few examples of men whining;

- A friend's kid got into 4 different accidents over time and it was "never his fault." It was always "those other drivers" fault. No mention that the kid already had 2 traffic tickets in the last 6 months. Dad was whining.
- Dad whined that his kid wasn't picked as a pitcher on his little league team, but neglected to mention that in the past season his kid was an absolute ace at first base and when he did pitch he stunk at it.
- "I can't land a job. I go out a couple of days a week and fill out applications but nobody calls." Sorry buddy, you've got to do better than that. You have to be relentless in your efforts to make it happen. A couple of days a week isn't going to happen.
- "My wife hasn't been saved. I keep praying for it to happen." Her getting saved is a deal between her and the Holy Spirit. When she is ready to let Him into her heart, He will come. The whiner's job is to lead by example by his own spiritual growth which he should be doing instead of whining about his wife.
- "None of the neighbors like us. They are just cold folks." Really? Maybe instead of looking at the one finger pointing at the neighbors, he should look at the 3 point back—at himself. Something's going on with how he shows himself to those neighbors.

Winners take personal responsibility for situations when they are whining situations. Winners know they are responsible only for their own actions, not those of others. Winners know those things he can handle and is responsible for. They also know that much of which they could whine about is really God's business. Winners focus on themselves and God, not on all the ills they see. Winners are secure, whiners are not. Winners wear big boy pants. Whiners still wear diapers.

Bottom Line Thought: Do you dodge your own responsibility in favor of whining?

Day 165:
Be Very, Very Careful

Let's play a little game of pretend for just a minute;

- You and your wife both smoke. You don't smoke in the house; you step out onto the porch. Nor do you smoke in the car. You both also make it a point to tell your kids how bad smoking is for them.
- You are driving to a local shopping center with your son so that you can teach him to drive in the unused areas of the parking lot. You're talking with him on the way about his future driving. You get pulled over by the police for not only running through a stop sign, but also for speeding.
- You talk to your children about the need to go to church. Your wife takes them every Sunday while you are out golfing with your buddies.
- You try to give the impression that you are serious about being a Christian, yet when a project you are working on doesn't come all together and the boss has indicated his displeasure, you go ballistic, and your language is definitely not nice.
- All of your friends have commented about how your family seems so nice, that it's nice to see a man so devoted to his wife and children. One day there is front page news in the local paper that you have been busted for possessing porn on your computer.

Is there a common thread throughout those pretend scenes? Of course there is. In each one, which could apply to any number of us, there are 2 different lives being lived—the one we want to project, and the one we really are.

When it comes to our efforts to be a witness to others, there is no room for two of us. There can only be one—the real man that we are if we are serious about or efforts. Others see who, and what, we really are. It is by that observation that they determine whether to trust us or not, just as their observation may be the only one that might cause them to come to Christ. We not only have to talk the talk, we have to walk the walk.

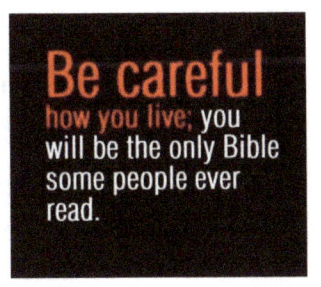

> **Be careful** how you live; you will be the only Bible some people ever read.

Bottom Line Thought: Are you very careful in every aspect of your life, knowing that you may well be the reason for someone being saved?

Day 166:
What Gets Lost

- It's a crowded house party, with plenty of kids running around and the television on for whoever might be interested. You're trying to talk some baseball over in a corner with a couple of buddies.
- It's a concert with a well known band and a whole bunch of people jamming to the tunes, many with a buzz-on, and very noisy. Your girlfriend is trying to say something to you.
- You get home from a nasty day at work. Even the traffic on the way home was terrible, and you are late. You're frazzled and worn out. You walk in the house and it's like walking into a jabber-fest. The kids are clamoring for your attention, and you wife seems to want to share every little detail about her boring day.

How much conversation gets lost in those scenes? How many "excuse me's" will get offered up because the person couldn't hear?

We Christians pray, don't we? Sometimes we do it in the quiet time in our home—say, for example, right before we go to bed. Do we ever wonder how much gets lost in the conversations wherev we pray? Probably more does than we realize.

You see, that's part of the problem with us sometimes. We are praying *to* God instead of *with* God, and when it's a one sided conversation, well, you bettcha, there is something that is going to get lost in that conversation! Perhaps we should start our prayer time like this;

> **"Lord, help me to listen to YOU in prayer
> as much as you listen to me. Amen**

I can't help but wonder, if we did that, what a conversation would be like when nothing gets lost, because we will really hear what He has to say. What might we be missing, and how might that change the way we see things and do things?

Bottom Line Thought: Here's a hard question—do you routinely pray to God or with God?

Day 167:
Yes

Yes, I'm a Christian.

Yes, I can be the biggest hypocrite ever.

I backslide.

I fall.

I stray onto the wrong path.

But—God is working in me.

I may be a mess, but I'm His mess.

And—He is slowly straightening me out.

The day will come when I will be at His side, His work in me done.

Until that day, I will take His hand, and let Him do in me what needs to be done.

Even if it's painful, it will be for me.

Because—when He is done, it will all be worth it.

Day 168:
Right Now

Many of us act as if we were born without the patience gene. Chances are, however, we were all born with it, we just suffer from PDS—Patience Deficiency Syndrome. One of the characteristics of that illness is, *I want it, and I want it NOW.*

Here are some of the things we do when we are afflicted by PDS;

- Unwise, or stupid, spending at inappropriate times.
    - We get our needs and wants mixed up.
- Inappropriate anger in driving situations.
    - We're always in a hurry—our fault, yes?
    - Drivers do dumb things—we can't fix stupid, yes?
- Allowing ourselves to keep arguments going to prove we're right.
- We expect God to hear our prayers and answer them now.
    - Check that, we more often demand it, right?
    - We get angry when He doesn't.

In my own family, some close to me aren't saved, nor do they have a relationship with Jesus. I have to be very careful because admittedly, I have PDS. I want them to be saved and accept Christ right now. It's easy for me to forget my own history when my mom and one of my daughters prayed for me for years and years. Neither expected it right then. They only expected that God would hear their prayers and in His time and in His way I would find my way. It happened. They didn't have PDS.

We will all eventually find that there is a strong antidote for PDS. It's called faith.
He wants us to keep praying.
When we keep praying, it builds our faith in Him.

Once we have that antidote, faith, "right now", amazingly, becomes radically less important as a driver in the way we do things. We take a back seat to God instead.

Bottom Line Thought: What will it be in your life—PDS or faith? I want your answer now!

Day 169:
Angel Of Apathy

When spring break comes the kids are out of school. I'd bet that a lot of them get bored and ask, "What's there to do?" A typical response from the mom may well be, "just go find something to do."

Us big kids get bored and restless as well, don't we? Even when our days are filled with the things we need to do in order to do life, we get those moments when we get bored once in a while. At those times it may be God nudging us to do something.

Matthew West sings a Christian Contemporary song titled *Do Something*. The lyrics address some of the ills of the world, and then the question is asked, "God, why don't you do something?" Perhaps that same thought rolls through our minds every so often as we open our eyes to the plight of others. After the question is asked, the next verse is the answer—"I did, I created you." Then the chorus is sung;

> *If not for us, then who*
> *If not me and you*
> *Right now, it's time for us to do something*
> *If not now, then when*
> *Will we see an end*
> *To all this pain*
> *It's not enough to do nothing*
> *It's time for us to do something*

As I listened to this powerful song recently, I was reminded of what a family I am very close to does regularly on Saturday afternoons. They make that time of their family life the time to do something—they prepare simple meals and take it to a small homeless encampment nearby and give the folks a meal. They do this very privately, with no publicity wanted—they do it because their hearts have led them there. They are NOT the *Angels of Apathy* sung about in the song.

Isn't it true that if we wanted to, we could find some small way to *do something*? We don't have to be *Angels of Apathy* do we? We can simply be another soldier of God's sharing and caring army in any number of ways. We only have to look for, or make, opportunities, and then choose to sign on.

Bottom Line Thought: If you are experiencing some nudges, maybe it's God's way of telling you you're and *Angel of Apathy* and He's recruiting for His care and share army. Why not?

Day 170:
I Ate The Whole Thing

"*I can't believe I ate the whole thing*." We've made that statement a time or two haven't we? I used it a while back after a trip to a great buffet. The line is from an advertising campaign for Alka Seltzer™ which came out years ago and was an instant hit because of the catchy line and the way they used it in the ads.

As men walking through our walks of life, no matter where we are in our spiritual journeys, we pray—at least once in a while. Those prayers can be anything from a good old fashioned foxhole prayer, to prayers of thanks and praise. Sometimes those prayers are very, very private, and at other times it may be with others in a group prayer.

When we are all by ourselves, and we're in "normal" times when the stuff isn't hitting the fan, when we're praying just to pray, how often do we fully dump ourselves into His lap? Do we share it all? Do we give all of our sin, not in general terms, but specific sins, over to Him? Or, do we hold back and offer it up in generalities?

If we're going to buy into the idea of prayer, why shouldn't we be all in? If we're not all in with our prayer lives, what's the point of doing it? It took me a long time to realize just how big God is, and that He is limitless with His people. Besides the benefits to our souls, hearts, and well-being, our *complete transparency* with God will never prompt Him to say "I can't believe I ate the whole thing." He can handle it all, and he wants to, because God is God and not Alka Seltzer™. Nothing, absolutely nothing, we share with Him in prayer will cause Him to love us any less.

Bottom Line Thought: If you were to take a thorough look at yourself, are there things you don't share with Him through prayer? Why not? Are you afraid He'll have to take some Alka Seltzer™?

Day 171:
If Those Walls Could Talk

Executive sessions about personnel, back rooms where politician's deals are made, the "talk" between the salesman and the manager of the auto dealership—all of those are times we wonder "if those walls could talk", what would they say? Each is a place we are not privy to, because the discussions may have some impact on us, yet we'd like to know what went on there. "If those walls could talk" runs through our minds.

The same thought occurs about friends, wives, our kids, and work cohorts when we sense they have put up walls. Our gut is screaming at us that something is going on that is uncomfortable for them. We ask if there is something happening that we should know, or what's bothering them, and we get something that should have a copyright on it—"oh, I'm fine." They're masking. They've thrown up walls, walls which are sometimes hard to penetrate.

Those folks aren't the Lone Ranger. Us guys are pretty darn good at building the same kind of walls aren't we? We're real good at it when it comes to emotions that show the soft side of us. We don't build walls around our explosive anger though, do we? We save the walls for those things (emotions, feelings, thoughts) that really matter to the ones around us.

Were it not for some Godly men who wondered what my walls would say if they could talk, I wouldn't be where I'm at in my spiritual journey today. God used those men to tear those walls apart. You see, God doesn't care about our walls because they don't stop Him. He knows what they would say and He knows, in His wisdom, that our walls prevent us from being all we can be. As long as we have those walls we will never be free, nor will we ever be the men God would love us to be.

We can all be men who, through love, patience, and understanding, can help other guys tear down those walls within them. So we should never wonder what Fred's walls would say if they could talk. If we're Godly men, we'll help him get rid of those walls so nobody has to wonder.

Bottom Line Thought: What kind of walls have you thrown up? What would they say? Are you open to the opportunity to help another man take his walls down?

Day 172:
George Carlin

Carlin was a stand-up comedian who could address the most common of life experiences in a very funny way. Many liked him, and many didn't. He certainly used language that inflamed some, and provoked wild laughter in others. In spite of his language, his keen perception of everyday things, from large to small, from the obvious to the subtle, provided him with an endless supply of materials for his shows. Here's a meme of his take on life.

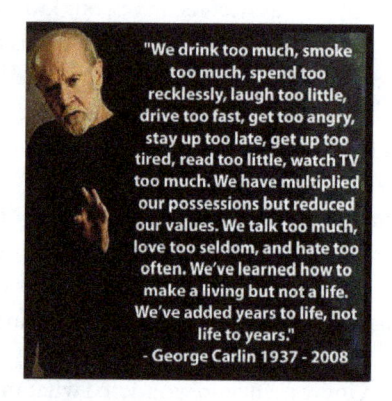

> "We drink too much, smoke too much, spend too recklessly, laugh too little, drive too fast, get too angry, stay up too late, get up too tired, read too little, watch TV too much. We have multiplied our possessions but reduced our values. We talk too much, love too seldom, and hate too often. We've learned how to make a living but not a life. We've added years to life, not life to years."
> - George Carlin 1937 - 2008

Suppose, for a moment, that George Carlin was a hugely successful Christian comedian delivering that talk about other Christians. He'd be talking some tall truth there, and it wouldn't be too funny would it? And, were he that successful Christian comedian, I wonder what else he might have added about things we neglect to do as Christians.

Bottom Line Thought: Do you see yourself in any of that bit by Carlin? If so, what effect are those things having on your relationships and your spiritual life?

Day 173:
Turn The Heat Down

"It's about progress, not perfection" is a comment I heard many times when sitting around tables with strangers in meeting rooms of church basements years ago. That mantra is a great guideline for those struggling with addiction. It serves as a gentle reminder that getting better is a process, not an event.

We tend to forget that it's no different in our spiritual journey. Being a Christian isn't an event—it's a process, a lifetime process at that. Contrary to what many of us think, it isn't about perfection. Our walk is about progress. Most of us know that we're not perfect, nor will we ever be. Yet we continue to beat ourselves up for not being perfect almost every time we do something contrary to what we know is God's will for us.

We play a huge role in our children's growth into young adults. Throughout the years from baby to twenties, we don't see flawless perfection. We see progress because their growth is a process full of ups and downs, trials and tribulations, missteps and mistakes, and most of all, positive learning from all of that. When our kids were growing up we weren't scorekeepers. We were forgivers as they made those stupid mistakes that they eventually learned from. We need to look at God in the same way as we struggle with our spiritual journey. He's no scorekeeper. He's a forgiver.

Let's turn the heat down. We tend to put a lot of extra heat on ourselves for screwing up. Instead of beating ourselves up over it, we need to look at whatever it was as a positive. It's a lesson to be learned from if we choose it to be, which is a real positive. In addition to turning the heat down, we need to take a moment to remember that there was only one perfect one. His name was Jesus. He knew of our imperfect nature and He died on the cross for us. He carried our sin, our mistakes, our imperfection, so that we could make progress toward the ultimate perfection. He handed us a process to live by, not on a silver spoon, but on a wood cross.

Bottom Line Thought: Are you a scorekeeper or a forgiver with your kids, wife, friends, *and* yourself? Do you grasp and embrace the concept of progress?

Day 174:
Irritants

"He always leaves the seat up on the toilet"

"She just can't seem to park the car straight in the garage"

"He leaves his desk at home such a mess all the time"

"The kid always leaves his bath towel on the floor"

Irritants are little things about others and what they do (or don't do) that fester within us and can slowly build up to anger. They aren't a reflection of the character of the "offending" person. They are simply irritants, things that "bug" us. They are no big deal. We know the earth won't stop spinning on its axis because of them. Yet, if we aren't careful, those little idiosyncrasies can become "big" things—to us.

It's easy to pick up on those little irritants and finally do or say something we later wish we could take back. I went to the kitchen to make a cup of coffee. On the counter was a spray bottle of lens cleaner. Its normal place is on a shelf a foot and a half away. However, almost every time it's used, it's left on the counter. It had become an irritant. As I muttered under my breath while I put the bottle away the other day, it dawned on me—it's *just* an irritant—nothing more, nothing less. And, it caused me to take pause and think—how many irritants am I responsible for (like, my messy desk)?

Don't we have a lot of better, more far reaching concerns than those little irritants to worry about? In my case, I couldn't help but think that there are a lot of things about me that I need to be concerned about instead of that little bottle of lens cleaner. Like, for instance, how I reacted to it in the first place—a touch of smug anger—"she didn't put it away again."

I'm pretty sure that if God were closely watching me He would find lots of irritants about me. Oh—He is watching me. I think I have some work to do. He doesn't let our irritants stand in the way of our relationship with Him. That's enough reason for us to *not* let the irritants of others stand in the way of our relationship with them. They just aren't worth it are they?

Bottom Line Thought: How do you react to those irritants that really don't amount to a hill of beans in the grand scheme of things?

Day 175:
A Tough Issue

I'm sure we've all been to at least one funeral service. To be honest, I don't like funerals. On the other hand, I love services called Celebrations of Life, because that's exactly what they are. There's a difference between the two—and it's often a glaring difference.

Frankly, I've been to some funerals for some pretty awful people—and that's *not* said in a judgmental way. In those cases, sadly, the deceased had absolutely no relationship with the Lord, and the lives they lived were a clear reflection of the lifestyle they chose. That said, I have never heard a Minister or Funeral Director speak the truth at one of those funerals. I've never heard something like;

"Sadly, Jack never embraced Christianity. Nor did he live a life which showed any indication that he understood what being a follower of Christ means. He seemed to care only about himself first, and his family last. He was known to chase around on his wife, and he was abusive toward his kids. He provided, but he was not a good husband or father."

Instead, at those services I've heard what seemed to me to be rather insincere efforts to offer the families and friends of the deceased some hope and feel good message that the deceased was indeed going to heaven. There is never any mention of the kind of life the person led—unless it is of their accomplishments that really have little bearing on their eternity.

At the Celebrations of Life services I've attended, the differences from a regular funeral are glaring. At the celebrations there is no doubt that the deceased had a fabulous relationship with the Lord, and that they led their life in service to the Lord and to others. There is never an iota of doubt that the person was truly loved, and that he impacted, in a very positive way, the lives of most who knew him. Lastly, there is, at those celebrations, a very dominant sense of joy among all present, a joy that comes from the knowledge that the deceased is indeed at the feet of Jesus in Heaven.

Bottom Line Thought: Since it is a known fact that we all die, do you prefer just a funeral or a Celebration of Life for your remaining family to remember you by? Are there changes you need to make so such a celebration can take place?

Day 176:
For The Women

What are some of the differences between a Christian guy and a Man of God?

1: A Christian guy might say he loves you. A Man of God will love God more than you, and you are secure with that.
2: A Christian guy might quote or text you Bible verses. A Man of God will have those verses written on his heart and will live them out.
3: A Christian guy might go to church. A Man of God will know that his highest calling is to give glory to God.
4: A Christian guy might "accidently" compromise your virtue. A Man of God will protect it above all else.
5: A Christian guy might be very attractive. A Man of God will have a beautiful heart regardless of how he looks.
6: A Christian guy might take you out. A Man of God will hold you up before God in his prayers.

Hey guys—how much time and effort do we needlessly waste trying to appear to be Christian guys instead of <u>being</u> Men of God? Aren't we sometimes a little too fanatical about how we appear to be, rather than how we really are? Could that be because we aren't truly Men of God yet?

Bottom Line Thought: Whether single or married, how do the differences between a Christian guy and a Man of God line up with who you are? Which one do others see in you?

Day 177:
Some Life-ism's

We're all businessmen of sorts. Our smile is our logo. Our personality is our business card. How we leave others feeling after an experience with us becomes our trademark.

Often, one of the most difficult things we can say is actually one of the most intelligent things we can say—"I don't know."

Whenever we become confronted with something new in our culture, we need to try a healthier approach—love it first, judge it later.

If we include "I'm available" everyday in our morning prayers, we will find ourselves becoming more openly available to what God has in store for us.

Live in the world. Don't hunker in the bunker. Live as a learner. We learn the most from people not like us.

He Looks Right Through Me

He looks right through me,

past my sin and the state I'm in.

He sees my heart and sets me free,

to be the man I'm meant to be.

So often when we're looking at our insides, we're looking at the wrong paycheck. Whenever we feel like we're falling apart, it's really God putting the pieces together. God is God, and I am not.

I've got to be a lower rower—more of a servant for others and a trustee of what I have.

Day 178:
Living Large

I ran into a new friend, Dean, at church a while back and asked him how he was doing. He gave me an answer I didn't expect when he said, "I'm living large." He said it with the same huge beautiful smile he gave me when I walked into the front door of the church for the very first time. I didn't expect that answer because I knew that he has had some significant medical issues. Here's something I know about Dean. He is truly living large, because what he meant by the term was that it is all the small good things about his life that fill it and have given him the ability to understand how much he is loved and blessed.

Couldn't all of us make that statement if we chose to? Are there any of us who can't see and appreciate all of those small insignificant things that we are blessed with? Do we want to allow just one or two things that may negatively affect us to control how we view life and cause us to be "down" or have a negative outlook? Isn't life more than that?

Without going into a litany of things that *could* cause me to be a legitimately negative person, let me share some of the small things in my life that make me know that I too am living large;

- Though we are unevenly yoked, and will never agree on some things, I have no doubt that my wife loves me.
- I have 7 kids who love me and never hold my past against me.
- I am not perfect, nor a perfect Christian, yet I know, without any doubt, that God loves me and stands by me, and my family respects me.
- I am not wealthy, nor even financially secure, yet I know I have all I need in life and I can willingly share what I have with needy others and my church.
- I am completely certain that despite myself I will one day live in Heaven and see those who have gone before me.

Living large is a state of mind that comes out of being secure in our own skin, our relationships, and in our faith. Christ followers are indeed living large.

Bottom Line Thought: Are you living large or are there things or thought processes that you need to change to get there?

Day 179:
Where Are You Going?

Who hasn't seen a dog chasing its tail? It's a humorous thing to watch as they run in repeated circles trying to catch that elusive tail. Then, when they have caught it, what happens? In a word—nothing, because they realize that the tail is just a part of them.

We humans have been known to chase our tails, figuratively, haven't we? We call it chasing circles or spinning in circles. Sometimes we go in circles so much that it seems as if we are in a spiral—a downward spiral. It doesn't feel good, because we begin to sense that there is no way out. Like that dog chasing his tail, all of our focus is on what it is that we are chasing and why we are chasing it. We are simply chasing the wrong things.

Our lives aren't meant to be that way. We weren't born to be like that. Chasing circles is something we do to ourselves. The circles we chase are *not* dictated by our circumstances. It is extremely hard to find any joy and peace in a life that is chasing circles.

There is nothing that matters more in our lives than the security of having a sense of joy, peace, and harmony, each of which comes from a committed relationship with Christ. With the faith that comes from that kind of relationship, it is difficult to begin chasing circles. There is only one place to go, and that is even closer to Him.

Spinning out of control and chasing circles isn't why God made us. He made us to be godly men, and He provided all of the instruction we need to become godly men. It's called the Bible.

Bottom Line Thought: Where are you going? Do you find yourself chasing circles or spinning out of control more than you would like? How does it make you feel about yourself? Why are you missing a sense of joy, peace, and harmony in your life? Do you really need to be like the dog chasing his tail?

Day 180:
Who Is He?

He didn't have any servants...
but they called Him Master.
He had no education..
but they called Him Teacher.
He had no medicines or medical degree...
but they called Him Healer.
He had no army...
yet kings feared Him.
He won no military battles...
but He conquered the world.
He committed no crime...
but they killed Him.
He was buried in a tomb...
yet He lives today.
We are totally unworthy of His love...
but He loves us more than we will ever know.
We are totally undeserving...
yet through His Word we are told repeatedly that He has prepared a place for us...
if only we believe that He died for our sins.
He is Jesus.
(Unknown author)

It's In Your Hands Now

TODAY

IS THE FIRST BLANK PAGE

OF <u>YOUR</u> NEW 365 PAGE BOOK.

WRITE A GREAT ONE

AND KNOW THAT GOD IS WITH YOU

ALL THE WAY !!

Epilogue

On March 24, 2015, my friend and mentor, Norm Whitney, left this world to be with Jesus. He succumbed, as he knew he would, to the cancer that ravaged his body. What the cancer never touched was his heart for the Lord and his friends, his belief that God is real, and his love for the Word.

This book started as a passing fancy, which turned into a daydream. Out of that arose some real thought, which morphed into a dream. The dream took on a life and evolved into work, which, in turn, became the reality that is this book. Thanks to the constant and faithful encouragement of Norm, the book was written.

On my last visit with Norm shortly before he passed he asked about this book, one he had such a hand in through his love for me and his praise for the effort. I explained that I was about half way through the manuscript at the time and he beamed his approval with one of his patented winks and a thumbs up.

On that visit, he shared some scripture, very encouraging scripture about facing troubles, tests, and hardships. He did this with each of his visitors in his last days as he continued to remain full of smiles, hugs, love, and encouragement for all of us.

May we all come to love the Lord as Norm did, and let our lights shine right up to the very end just as he did.

Thank you, Norm, for being such a godly pal.

CPSIA information can be obtained
at www.ICGtesting.com
Printed in the USA
LVHW080145150123
736970LV00002B/26

9 781498 438223